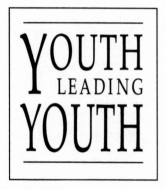

YOUTH
LEADING
YOUTH

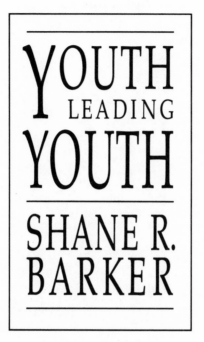

YOUTH LEADING YOUTH

SHANE R. BARKER

Deseret Book Company
Salt Lake City, Utah

To my parents

©1987 Shane R. Barker
All rights reserved
Printed in the United States of America

No part of this book may be reproduced in any
form or by any means without permission in writing
from the publisher, Deseret Book Company,
P.O. Box 30178, Salt Lake City, Utah 84130.
Deseret Book is a registered trademark of
Deseret Book Company.

First printing November 1987

Library of Congress Cataloging-in-Publication Data

Barker, Shane R.
  Youth leading youth.

  Includes index.
  1. Youth—Religious life.   2. Church work with youth—
Mormon Church.   3. Christian leadership—Mormon Church.
I. Title.
BX8643.Y6B37   1987   259'.2   87-22347
ISBN 0-87579-111-5

CONTENTS

1

RUNNING WITH THE BALL
You Can Be the Leader

Time! Time out!"

The captain of the Red Raiders, the best basketball team in the eighth grade, gestured frantically toward the nearest official.

"Come on, ref! Time out!"

The referee, caught looking at the scoreboard, finally whistled the clock dead.

"Time out, red!" he shouted.

I felt a surge of excitement as the Raiders left the floor. There were just eleven seconds left on the clock, and we were ahead by one point. For the first time all season, we had a chance to beat them!

Steve Birrell, our team captain, was chattering like a squirrel as we ran off the court.

"We've got 'em, Shane! We've really got 'em! We're gonna *win* this game!"

I felt another rush of excitement as we joined the

huddle. Steve said we were going to win. And I believed him.

Steve had said all along we could do it. "We're a good team," he told us before the game. "But they won't be up for us. If we go out there and play like we mean it, we can take 'em."

If anyone but Steve had said that, we would have laughed. After all, the Raiders were the best team in the eighth grade. They had the tallest players in the league, and they had the best shooters. Besides that, the Raiders had beaten us every time we played them that season. To suddenly start thinking about beating *them* wasn't very realistic. But Steve convinced us that we could do it.

Steve was our team leader. When he came fired up for a game, the rest of us were fired up, too. When he played like the next three or four minutes would determine the outcome of the entire season, the rest of us played that way, too. If he told us we could win a game — even against the Red Raiders — we believed him.

And Steve proved that he meant exactly what he said. He opened up the game with three quick baskets from the top of the key. He made two steals that we converted to points on the fast break. He played with an intensity that fired us up and rattled our opponents.

And now, with eleven seconds left and our biggest game of the season on the line, he was still pumping us up.

"We've been stopping them all afternoon," he said. "We can do it for another eleven seconds. All we have to do is keep 'em outside the line."

Steve made it sound easy, but he had already shown us that we could do it. We had no reason to doubt it. And we played the next eleven seconds like the Boston Celtics in the final game for the world championship. We beat the only team that really mattered to us.

The funny thing was, Steve wasn't our best player. He

wasn't our tallest player. He wasn't even our highest scorer. But he was our team leader.

One week he had an ear infection, and so the doctor wouldn't let him come to school. We had two games that week, and we lost both of them. We didn't lose because Steve wasn't there to score points for us. We lost because Steve wasn't there to give us the boost we needed to play our best.

You probably know people like Steve. People who can motivate and inspire others. People who can take charge of a group. People who can lead others to be their very best.

You can be one of them.

I know a young woman who was the president of her high school debate team. Marci was a fine debater, and she was a superb leader. She made each person on the team want to win. She showed such interest in each one that every person felt important. She made each person feel that the team was nothing without him or her. Before meets, Marci went to every practice round. She spent time with every person, watching, helping, and making suggestions. When things went wrong, she encouraged her teammates. When things went right, she praised them.

Marci helped people because she made it clear that she was interested in *them*. To her, the team was only second.

Now maybe you've been called to lead the deacons quorum. Maybe you're the Laurel president. Or maybe you're the mission's newest zone leader. Then you have the opportunity to bless and guide those you serve. You can draw from them a best they've never dreamed of and give them a glimpse of their own destiny.

Think back to great leaders you've had. They were probably able to lead you as if they had laid a magic hand on your shoulder. They drew from you a best that you never thought possible. Many of them were probably just your age.

When I was in high school, a friend of mine named Melody asked me to write a play for the senior class assembly. She was the student body secretary, and she knew I loved to write.

"You've got just the personality we need for this," she said. "You could write us the best play ever."

I wasn't so certain. I loved to write, but I wasn't sure I could write anything as great as what Melody wanted.

"Yes, you can!" she said. "I've read your stories. You write with more life and energy than anyone I know. If you write the play, it'll be the best one we've ever had!"

By the time Melody had finished talking, I believed her. She had convinced me that the school needed me. She made me believe that unless I wrote the play, the whole thing would be a flop. So when I finally sat down to write it, I was determined to do the very best job I possibly could. Melody had drawn from me a best I didn't know I had.

You can do the same thing for someone else.

Most of the groups you work with will have fine adult leaders. And that's great. They can give you lessons and advice from their own experiences. Learn from them as much as you can. But remember that on many teams there are players who are leaders as much as the coach is. And you need them! Just as coaches can't get out in the game and play, your adult leaders can't always get out in the middle of the action either.

But you can! You can get right out on the floor and take charge. You can inspire, encourage, and motivate those around you. Decide now that you'll do it!

When I was in high school I had a friend named Bret who played on the football team. Bret was a defensive lineman who had a chest like a barrel and fingers like frankfurters. He wasn't fast, and he wasn't coordinated, but he could plow into an offense like a team of horses. Trying to stop him was like trying to stop a bulldozer with a hankie.

One time we were playing the team from a rival school.

It was late in the fourth quarter, and we were behind by a field goal. The other team had the ball third and four on our forty-five-yard line. At the snap, their quarterback dropped back to pass as Bret charged over the line on a blitz. The quarterback darted to the side and began his pass just as someone else ran into him. The ball shot straight up into the air . . . and came straight down into Bret's beefy hands.

Now Bret had never in his life held the ball on an offensive play. He had smothered fumbles and blocked for teammates on interceptions. But he had never carried the football.

That didn't bother him. Like the most seasoned rusher in the Super Bowl, Bret tucked the ball under his arm and ran with it. He probably would have made a touchdown, too, except that nearly every player on the other team was able to catch up with him to help drag him to the ground.

The point is that Bret didn't hesitate when his time came. He was strictly a defensive player, but when his chance came, he didn't waste time worrying about his ability or experience. He didn't stop to call for help. He took the ball and ran with it.

You can do the same thing. You can take your call to leadership and run with it. You can use *your* talents, drive, and energy to make your group the best it can be. You can give the people you lead a glimpse of their own destiny. You can show them the quality of success.

And it doesn't matter if you're just twelve years old. It doesn't matter if you're thirteen, fourteen, or fifteen. It doesn't matter if you're the newest elder or sister in the mission. As a young person, you have all the energy and enthusiasm you need to be a tremendous leader.

Not only that, but by starting out young, you can start out right. You can develop now good, solid skills of leadership that will carry you far into your adult life.

During a recreation class, a teenage girl named Nicole

stood at the edge of a cliff. She was supposed to rappel to the bottom, but she was nervous about trying. As Brandon — a boy in the class her own age — secured a safety line around her, she said, "I can't do this."

Brandon smiled at her. "Of course you can!" he said. "You just don't know how yet!"

And then, with terrific patience, support, and understanding, Brandon taught her how to get to the bottom safely. He gave Nicole the confidence to try.

People you know need leaders like Brandon. They need leaders who are able to teach them the principles of success. They need leaders who can give them the confidence to become their very best.

They need — you!

Things to Do Now!

- Decide to be a leader. Tell yourself every day, "I am a leader!"

- Take advantage of your youth. As a young person you have great energy and enthusiasm. Use them to fire up the groups you lead.

- Promise never to be average! Strive to be your best always. When you set out to do something, don't just try to get it done. Instead, do it the best it can be done. Encourage those you lead to do the same.

2

How to Build a Raft
Forming the Group

Y ou want us to do what?"

I looked over the knot of boys and pointed toward the dock anchored halfway across the small lake. I spoke matter-of-factly.

"I want you to build a raft, paddle it out to the dock, and bring me the can that's sitting out there."

The boys—all of them twelve- and thirteen-year-old Boy Scouts—exchanged worried glances. Micah, a boy with sandy hair, looked up hopefully.

"Why can't we just swim out to it?" He glanced at the other boys. "I could do that."

A couple of the others nodded their support and moaned when I shook my head.

"Sorry. The can contains a sensitive payload that must stay absolutely dry. The only way to keep it from getting wet is to build a raft."

I paused a moment for emphasis, and then pointed down the shore to where three other groups of Scouts were having similar conversations.

"There is a hitch," I said. "We're going to be racing those other patrols. Only the winning team will get to keep the prizes inside the can."

At the idea of a race, the Scouts became a little more enthusiastic. I led them down to the beach where I had stacked a pile of logs and poles, several lengths of rope, and four styrofoam rolls that would keep the raft buoyant.

"It doesn't matter how you build the raft," I explained. "To win the race, all you have to do is get out to the dock, get the can, and bring it back without getting it wet."

The Scouts were finally getting excited, and once they all were ready and the signal to begin was given, they took off like a pack of hounds.

That was the beginning of a week-long Boy Scout leadership course. The boys were there to learn the skills they needed to lead their troops at home.

After arriving at camp, the Scouts had been organized into groups of five or six. Care was taken to see that no one was placed in a patrol with anyone he already knew. Being with a group of strangers was an important part of this first-day's activities.

Once my group began working on their raft, I just sat back and watched. Carefully. I wasn't interested in how they built their raft, but I did want to see how they went about doing it. Right off the bat, a boy named Wade began taking charge. The other boys followed his lead. Wade wasn't the oldest Scout in the bunch, and he wasn't the biggest. But he did have a dynamic, energetic personality that made him *seem* like an authority.

"You guys start sorting out the rope," he said, singling out two boys standing to his left. "And the rest of us will get going on the raft."

But Wade wasn't the only leader in the group. As the boys bent into their work, Micah took a step back and began looking things over. He glanced down the bank to where the rival patrols were busy lashing away, then called to Wade.

"Look," he said, "the way we're going we're going to

have a good raft, but we won't have any place to lash the styrofoam. We ought to get a couple of guys to lash all the styrofoam together, then when the raft's done, we could just lay it on top and tie it on tight."

Wade took only a moment to decide. "Good idea. Do you want to do it?"

"Sure."

"Okay. Get someone to help you, and go ahead."

Within a short time, the raft was finished. Actually, it was almost finished. But when a rival patrol began pushing their craft into the lake, Wade decided that enough was enough, and he had the gang shove off. It was a close race, and the other patrol might have won. They reached the dock first and were on their way back when Micah remembered an important stipulation: the winning team had to bring the can back dry! In the resulting water fight, the can and all of the candy it contained were sunk, but the boys had such a good time that no one really cared.

The purpose of this activity was not really to see who could get to the dock first. It wasn't to see who could build the best raft. It was to give the boys a common goal and get them working together. By the time they were finished, they had all learned to rely upon one another. They had learned the importance of working together. They had become united.

Now, you may be putting a group together, too. Or maybe you're taking charge of a group that's already been formed. Either way, you'll need to form the group into a good, cooperative unit before it will be able to work effectively.

How do you do that?

In three ways. First, you've got to get everyone moving together. Second, you've got to let everyone help. And third, you've got to make the group *feel* like a group.

Sound complicated? It really isn't. Let's take a look at each of the three steps and see just what's involved.

First, get everyone moving together.

I was visiting a junior high school not too long ago and

got caught in the halls between classes. One minute I was walking freely down the hall, and the next I was trapped in the middle of hundreds of bustling students.

The trouble was, they were all going the other way. And I couldn't make any progress down the hall. Finally I just turned around and went the same way as everyone else. Suddenly everything was easier.

When you get everyone moving together — working toward the same goals — everyone will be helping everyone else along. The work will become easier.

Before the start of the season, a girls' volleyball team met outside the gym one afternoon. Out on the lawn was a circular platform two feet across and eighteen inches high.

"We're not going in to practice today," the coach said, "until we can get every person on the team *on* the platform."

"All at the same time?"

The coach nodded. "All at the same time."

If you have a ruler handy, try seeing just how big a two-foot circle is. And then imagine trying to get fifteen girls on top of it all at the same time.

It wasn't easy, but it was fun. The girls were soon crawling on top of one another, holding on to each other as if they had jumped out of an airplane with just one parachute. By the time they succeeded in getting all fifteen girls onto the tiny platform, everyone was laughing and giggling and anxious to try it again. More important, they understood when the coach asked, "Now, do you see the importance of teamwork?"

You'll find that when everyone is working together, the jobs you do will get done easier. Everyone will have more fun doing them. And the harder everyone is working, the harder it will be for anyone to try straying off.

Second, let everyone help.

A boys' club once went camping in the high Uintah

Mountains of northern Utah. They planned on hiking in to a remote mountain lake for three days. Their leaders arranged for a number of horses to pack in all their gear.

Things should have worked out well, but most of the boys had brought far too much gear, and the horses were loaded down heavily. So while their leaders hiked slowly along with the horses, the boys scampered on up the mountain.

Once they reached their camping spot, the boys scattered. A couple of them went fishing. Others went exploring. One of them began hunting arrowheads.

After a couple of hours, though, their leaders had still not arrived with the horses. A few of the boys became nervous. They worried that maybe they had hiked to the wrong lake. Some thought they must be lost. As the worries sank in, tempers began to flare. Finally a boy named Bruce took control.

"Listen," he said. "Maybe we're lost, and maybe we're not. But arguing isn't going to change things."

"So what do you want us to do?" someone sneered. "Sit around and play jacks?"

Bruce ignored the sarcasm. "If we're lost, then we'd better start doing something about it."

"Like finding our way out?"

Bruce shook his head. "No. If we are lost, it'll be best if we stay put. But we ought to get ready to spend the night if we have to. You know, build a shelter, find something to eat . . . "

The boys were instantly excited. "Yeah!" one agreed. "Let's build a shelter!"

"And I'll catch some fish for dinner," said another.

Bruce quickly organized the boys into teams. One began collecting wood and started a fire. Another set to work on a shelter. And two boys were sent back to the lake to try catching a few more fish for dinner. Everyone had something to do.

It wasn't long before the boys' leaders showed up with

the horses. They hadn't been lost, just a lot slower than they'd expected. But Bruce proved an important point. By getting everyone moving in the right direction and by letting everyone help, he kept everyone busy. He channeled their energy in a positive direction.

In the group you lead, make sure that everyone has a job to do. Keep the group members' energy channeled in a positive direction. By keeping them involved, you'll make them feel important to the group.

Third, make them feel like a group.

All people have a need to belong. They have a need to succeed. So let them know that they're part of something great.

When I was in the high school band, I played trumpet with a boy named McKay. He was one of the best high school musicians in the state, and he was our section leader.

Now, our director was a wonderful musician. He was a fine teacher who could tap more work from us than anyone else I've ever played for. He gave us pride as a band.

But McKay went a step further. He showed us what a great trumpet section could really be like.

"Let's all come in right after lunch," he suggested one day. "Then we can all be warmed up and tuned up by the time class starts."

McKay was asking us to give up part of our lunch break. There were a couple of us who didn't want to do that, but McKay just said, "Fine. Come in when you can."

The rest of us, though, showed up the next day halfway through lunch. We spent a few minutes warming up, then McKay tuned us up.

"All right," he said, finally. "Let's play some trumpets!"

For the next ten minutes we played the wildest pep tunes in our folders. The next day we were back again.

The best thing was that we were all improving our musical skills. But we were also developing pride as a team. By the time class started, we were all set and ready to go. We knew we were a step ahead of the rest of the class, and that made us feel good.

We also made up a trumpet section theme song, and we played it whenever our director stopped for a break or whenever we went to ball games. It was great fun.

Every one of us was proud to be a member of the trumpet section. McKay had given us something great to belong to. And we loved it.

Not only that, but other brass sections began doing the same things we did. Some started showing up during lunch to warm up. Others made up theme songs like ours. McKay's example was spreading.

But McKay wasn't finished. "The drummers are starting to copy us," he said one day. "We've got to figure out something we can do to stay on top."

"How about ties?" someone asked. "We could all wear ties to class."

"Perfect," McKay said. "Nobody wears ties to school. We'll be the first."

And we were. Not only did we stand out through our excellence, but we stood out through our appearance as well. We were untouchable.

McKay did great things for us that year. He showed us how great we could be. He showed us how much fun we could have. He gave us the motivation and the desire to be our best. He gave us reasons to achieve.

Make your group exciting to belong to. Establish a tradition of excellence that every group member will be proud of. You'll find that all of them will respond with increased support and loyalty. Most important, you'll find the power to lead them and change their lives.

Things to Do Now!

- Get the members of your group all moving in the same direction. Set goals they can work on together. Or find a contest they can attempt as a team. Let the heat of competition mold them together.

- Make sure that everyone is a part of the team. Make sure that everyone has a job. Find ways to keep even the youngest, least skilled members involved and active. Let them know that the group can't succeed without them.

- Develop pride in your group! Make the group exciting to belong to. Let them all know that they belong to something really great!

3

LOOKING FOR DIFFERENCES

Learning Each Person's Needs and Traits

Fourteen-year-old Steve Hilton punched the throttle as he rounded the bend, pushing hard for more speed. His snowmobile shot down the trail in a spray of snow.

"Hang on!" he shouted over his shoulder. "A lot of bumps coming up!"

An instant later the snowmobile hit the first dip. It pounded the icy whoop-de-doos like it was shooting over a flight of stairs, sending bursts of snow into the sky with every bump. The next second it was high in the air as it blazed over a jump.

"Wow!" Steve shouted again. "That's the best ride we've had yet!"

David Blacker, perched precariously on the back, wasn't so sure. His idea of snowmobiling fun was driving through deep powder and around tight, tricky turns. He liked technique more than speed. Riding with Steve made him edgy and nervous.

And Steve didn't like David's dizzying spins and turns. He liked flat, open stretches of road where he could open the throttle wide.

The two boys were riding partners on a seventy-mile trek through Yellowstone National Park. They decided before starting out that they would take turns driving and would switch places after every five miles. The first thing they learned was that when Steve was at the wheel they covered ground at breakneck speed, hitting every bump and jump he spotted along the way.

As soon as David took over, the ride became slower but was no less thrilling. Waiting until the last moment to spin around sharp corners, David could punch the sled into such a fishtail that Steve was certain he was going to be thrown off.

Even though Steve and David were best friends, neither of them liked riding with the other. Their styles of driving were too different.

As you look over the group you lead, you'll notice that no two people are alike. Just like Steve and David, every person will have his or her own likes and dislikes, traits and characteristics. What's fun for one may not be fun for another. To be an effective leader, you'll need to deal with this variety of personalities. That is one of the greatest challenges of leadership.

I have two friends from Ireland who ran for Brigham Young University and became All-Americans. Carey, a world-class marathoner who ran in the 1984 Olympics, loved the distances. She thought nothing of going out for a ten- or fifteen-mile run, and she once told me that she'd rather slosh through miles of mud and snow than train on an indoor track.

Aisling, on the other hand, shook her head at any distance longer than a mile, and she loved pounding the hardwood of indoor tracks. She won the mile run in the 1983 NCAA Indoor Championships, and she went undefeated in the sprints that entire season.

At first glance, the two runners seemed identical. They were both from Ireland, they were both All-Americans, and they both loved running. But where track was concerned, the similarities ended. They were actually as different as night and day.

In the group you lead, you'll find people who are just as different. But like the coaches who trained Carey and Aisling, don't be too quick to judge them. Don't expect sprinters like Aisling to like the distances or be good at them. And don't force marathoners like Carey to master the sprints.

Being able to plan around people's strengths and weaknesses is a skill that will set you apart as a leader. It isn't always easy, but the better you know each person, the better you'll be at it.

When I was a missionary in Japan, my mission president once called me and another elder into his office.

"We're going to open a branch in a city where we've never had missionaries before," he told us. "And it's important that we establish the work there as quickly as possible."

The president said he was assigning Elder Fox and me to work as companions in the new city, and he explained why he had chosen us.

"Elder Barker, you are one of the best investigator-finders in the mission. You have a special talent for sparking interest in the gospel among the people you meet."

I nodded. I was never sure exactly how I was able to do it, but I taught a great many people. But I was slow in the way I presented my lessons. I was almost always transferred before my investigators were ready for baptism.

Elder Fox was just the other way around.

"You never have more than a handful of investigators

at a time," the president reminded him. "But you baptize the ones you find very quickly."

So he put the two of us together. And what a team we made! In the eight weeks we worked together, we established in that small mountain town a branch that's still going strong today.

When you find someone in your group with obvious weaknesses, it's easy to be unhappy with him. After all, he's probably not working the way you want him to. And many leaders will simply try to change him.

But if you really want to be effective, learn to focus on his strengths. He's certain to have some. So find ways for him to contribute in the way he does best. Is he a terrible organizer? Maybe he's a terrific artist. Does she have a scratchy singing voice? Maybe she's a skilled pianist. Find out!

Just as everyone has different traits, everyone has different needs, too. I once took a group of teenage boys deep into the backcountry of southern Utah. We were preparing for a week-long outdoor leadership course, but the night after we arrived, a heavy rainstorm washed away all the roads leading onto the mountain. As soon as I learned we were stranded, I used the radio-telephone at Mt. Holly Ski Resort to phone my employer.

"I want you off the mountain as soon as possible," he said. "Drive as far as you can, then hike the rest of the way out. I'll have someone in town pick you up."

I didn't want to leave, but I had no choice. So I called everyone together and explained that we had a long hike ahead of us.

"I don't know how long it'll be before we're back," I said. "So make sure you pack up everything you're going to need."

I began by loading my backpack with notebooks, climbing equipment and other things I was sure I wouldn't be able to live without. Many of the items I packed were heavy, but they were important enough to me that I was willing to carry them.

After I was finished I went to help the others. The first thing I noticed was the difference in what everyone was taking. Justin, my chief ranger, was taking only the bare minimum of clothes, reserving most of the space in his pack for his rock- climbing gear. Jeff was busy padding his collection of cassette tapes. Roger was trying to figure out the best way to pack his fishing gear.

It didn't matter to me what the boys took. After all, it was their packs, their backs. And even though some of their selections seemed silly to me, I knew better than to interfere. No matter how much room they took, I knew Devon would be miserable without his wood-carving knives. No matter how heavy it was, I knew Evan couldn't live without his radio.

Every person's needs are different. And to realize their full potential in the group, group members will need to feel that their individual needs are being met. That is the first, best way to make them all feel that the group is working for *their* good, too.

Imagine for a moment being left-handed. Then suppose you went to a school that provided only desks with right-handed arm rests (you probably do!) or right-handed baseball gloves. Wouldn't you feel left out? Wouldn't you feel angry? And wouldn't you have every right to feel that way?

You bet you would! And that is why you must take each person's needs into account when you begin planning any project.

A dance teacher named Linda was once preparing a team of young dancers for a recital. Most of her dancers were high school and college age, but many of them were less than ten years old.

Teaching such different age groups was difficult. The older dancers wanted time and instruction to perfect their routines. The younger dancers needed practice, mostly, but their young bodies weren't yet capable of doing hard routines over and over again.

And so, while the older dancers were rehearsing, Linda took the younger ones into another room where she had them lie on the floor. Then she dimmed the lights, turned on the music, and asked the children to think through the dance in their minds, picturing every step and move.

It was a good trick. And it gave the children a chance to practice even when their young bodies couldn't dance any more.

Remember the people's emotional needs are just as important as their physical ones. One person in the group may be timid or shy. He'll need encouragement. The person beside him may lack self-confidence. She'll need opportunities to realize her strengths. Someone else may not feel liked. He'll need friends. And there may be someone who needs a lot of freedom. You may need to give her room to work.

When you begin to plan and provide for each person's needs, they will all begin to feel like they are each an important part of the group. They'll feel that the group is working for them, too. They'll respond with greater enthusiasm for the things you do. And they'll return your effort with increased respect and loyalty for you as their leader.

Things to Do Now!

• Make a list (like the example) of every person you lead. Now list one positive word (musician, scholar, athlete, and so on) that best describes each person. Don't use the same word for more than one person.

• Beside each person's name, list three traits that make

that person different from everyone else. (Does he like spinach? Can she play the oboe?)

- Now, beside each person's name, list three needs that person might have. (Does he need friends? Does she need to keep active?)

- Find ways to meet the needs of everyone in the group. Find ways to let each one know that he or she is an important part of the group.

Name/Description	Traits	Needs
Trent/Scholar	Shy, likes music, likes movies, plays clarinet, likes to read	Friends, lots of attention, time to be alone

4

BREAKING RECORDS
Working toward a Goal

4:07:08.

They looked like ordinary numbers. But anyone who knew James Allen knew they were more than that. He had them printed on the top of his school books, and he wrote them in the margins of his papers. He had them marked across his mirror at home, and he had them written over his bed. He even had them inked across the top of his running shoes.

The time of 4:07:08 just happened to be the state high school record in the mile run. It had been for thirteen years. And James was determined to break it.

"All my life I've wanted to be first, best, or fastest at something," he said. "And track was my best thing. The mile was my best distance. I wanted to know that I had run as fast as I possibly could."

James had set his goal early in his junior year. It was a tough goal, and it was one that he knew would take a lot of work. But he also knew that if he dedicated himself to it he *could* do it.

"It took me a whole year," he said. "I had to give up a lot of parties and movies to train. But I *wanted* that record. It was important to me. I had to prove I could do it."

James' goal motivated him all season long. It kept him going when times got hard. It drove him on when other failures threatened to discourage him. It gave him something to work for.

Then late in the year, James broke the record, lowering the time to 4:07:05. Doing it gave him a burst of exhilaration and confidence. It taught him the power of his own potential.

Goals can work the same magic on the group you lead. They can generate confidence. They can pull your group closer together. They can give the team a sense of purpose and accomplishment. And when the group finally meets a tough goal, everyone feels great. It's tough to beat the excitement of reaching a difficult goal.

I live near a high school that used to have the best debate team in the state. After winning the state championship for two years in a row, the team officers worried about what *new* goal they could reach for. And then someone had an idea.

"Let's see if we can go the entire year without losing a meet!"

At first everyone frowned: going undefeated was a pretty optimistic goal. But the more they let the idea sink in, the better it sounded. A whole year without losing a single meet! They decided to do it.

Many athletic teams often set the same goal. After all, no one likes to lose. But to this debate team, going undefeated was more than just an idle wish. It was a real goal.

Beginning even before the first day of school, the team began meeting to share ideas and study together. Every person was given research assignments. Experienced debaters coached less skilled teammates in practice. The whole team spent extra hours in practice.

Brad, who was a senior that year, said the team worked harder that season than ever before. Morale on the team was high. Every person felt needed. Every person felt important. And as the season progressed — and the team continued to win — everyone grew closer together.

The goal of going undefeated so permeated the team that every person wanted to do his or her very best. Every person put in hours of extra study and practice. It would have been easy to slack off, but no one did. The team's goal was too important to them.

By the time of the state meet, the team hadn't lost a single tournament. Everyone's confidence was high. The team had practiced and drilled one another time and time again. They knew what tactics their opponents were likely to try, and they were ready for them. There wasn't much anyone could spring on them that they weren't prepared for. And when they won, they were so excited they were all ready to go out and do it all over again.

Whenever people achieve a worthy goal, they talk about it for months and years to come. They bubble over it, tell stories about it, write their friends about it, and — best of all — they want to do something like it again!

Goals have great power to motivate people. They can pump a group full of excitement. And when the goals are properly chosen, they can provide great stamina and stimulation. A good goal can bring your group to life.

A Scout troop once planned a trip to the Great Lakes Canoe Base in Michigan. Each Scout needed more than $400 to make the trip, and none of them had anywhere near that much money. So they began a series of fundraising projects. And they were clever about it. They divided into patrols and had contests to see which patrol could earn the most money in a given week or month.

They had video parties for the winners, inviting the rival patrols to come too (as long as they brought the refreshments).

Now, if you've ever done fund-raisers, you know how dull they can be. But this troop was creative. One patrol organized a basketball hoop shoot. Each boy committed to shooting free throws for exactly thirty minutes, then found sponsors who would donate a penny for every shot he made in that half hour. On the day of the shoot, Scouts and sponsors crowded into the gym to watch. Patrol members sold pop, popcorn, and hot dogs. And in less than an hour, the patrol made more than $300.

A different patrol scrubbed oil stains from people's driveways. Another cut firewood. They strained their imaginations looking for new ways to earn money.

Each week the troop treasurer collected the money and announced the week's winning patrol. Each Friday night the boys had video parties. Their Scoutmaster kept the goal of $400 per Scout fresh in everyone's mind. And the closer they came to making it, the more excited everyone became.

In addition, the weekly video parties made great short-term goals. Each patrol wanted to be the one to win that week. When they did win, they wanted to do it again (it feels great when you win contests, doesn't it?). And when they didn't win, they resolved to do better the next week.

They had so much fun that inactive Scouts began coming to help out! (How many times have you seen inactive Scouts come to fund-raisers?)

By late July, three weeks before the trip, the troop had more than enough money for everyone to make the trip. The best part was that the troop stalwarts weren't the only ones going. The fund-raising had become so much fun and was so successful that even a couple of inactive Scouts — the ones who became active helping with fund-raisers — went too.

A well-planned goal had brought the entire bunch to life.

Without goals it's impossible to measure progress. And without goals it's difficult to motivate those you work with. People need goals to guide their work. They need objectives to work toward.

A high school trumpet player named Kelly worked for weeks trying to hit a high C. That's a note that's not called for very often, but high school trumpet players love high notes. They put fire and sparkle into pep tunes. And they're great fun.

Kelly's band liked to play a lively jazz tune at ball games and pep rallies that called for a high C. So the trumpet section decided it would be awesome if every player could hit and hold that note all at the same time.

A couple of the players could already do it. Kelly was one who couldn't. And so he worked on it over and over again. He spent time every day on drills that improved his range. It wasn't very much fun, but the thought of standing on the bleachers with his friends and belting out a high C drove him on.

Then one day it came. Doing triad drills he hit the note and held it. Then he did it again. He missed it the third time, but Kelly didn't care. He had done it!

With more work, practice, and endless drills, the high C became easier. And finally Kelly played it all the time. It was his favorite note. Not many musicians have favorite notes, but Kelly certainly did. The high C had taken too much work not to love it.

A dancer named Carrie had a similar experience. She belonged to a dance club, and she set the goal of doing a triple turn in her first recital.

"I had friends in the club who could do triple turns," Carrie said. "And I wanted to be as good as they were."

It took a lot of work. At first, Carrie couldn't even do a double turn without falling. But after much practice, she finally learned to do a double, and then she set her sights on the triple.

"I fell all the time," she said. "But I never gave up. I just kept working and trying. It took about three weeks, but then one day I did it! I felt so good that I did them all day."

Next time you're with a bunch of friends, try asking them what they're doing tonight. Or tomorrow night. Ask them what they're doing this weekend. And see how many of them say, "I don't know." Try it. Count how many of them don't have any particular plans for the future. Many people are like that their entire lives. They never decide where they're going. And because they don't know where they're going, they never get anywhere.

A group without goals is the same way. It has no reason for even existing. By setting goals, you create objectives for your group to work toward. Your goals will guide you through rough times. They'll motivate you through hard times. And they'll sustain you through difficult times.

When you begin setting goals, remember these suggestions:

First, let everyone help. After all, what's important to you should also be important to them. And make certain everyone knows what the group's goals really are. When everyone knows exactly what they're working toward, they'll never question what's going on or why you're doing the things you are.

Second, be specific. Don't just decide to be a better basketball team. (How do you measure a goal like that?) Instead, decide to spend an extra hour a week in practice. Decide to buy snappier uniforms. Decide to raise the team's foul- shooting to 75 percent. That way you'll never have any question about when you've reached your goals.

Third, set goals that make you stretch. But don't make them so unrealistic that they're impossible. A goal that requires no effort does no good. Neither does a goal that can't be reached. But goals that require extra work, thought, and dedication will spark new life in the group. Goals that offer a challenge will reward you with thrills that are hard to match.

Fourth, keep your goals in mind. Since the purpose of goals is to inspire the group, make sure they're doing their job! Evaluate your progress often. Let everyone know how things are shaping up. Let everyone share in the excitement that builds as you come closer and closer to your objective.

Fifth, be sure your goals are recorded somewhere. That makes them official. It keeps them from being forgotten. And it will let your goals nag you until you reach them. And that's the most important reason of all!

These suggestions apply to an individual's goals, too. As a leader, you should set a few personal goals to guide *your* work. Decide, for instance, to organize an agenda for next week's meeting. Or decide to keep a journal of your experiences with the group.

Let goals work their magic on you. Let them pump life and energy into the group you lead. As you do, you'll give everyone a sense of purpose and accomplishment. You'll build pride and unity. And you'll create excitement in your group that you never dreamed possible.

Things to Do Now!

• Make a list of your personal leadership goals. Decide now to bring Charlie back into the quorum. Or resolve to say something positive to each member of the group every day. Commit now to achieving those goals!

• Make goals that are specific. Don't just decide to be a better leader. Instead — for instance — promise to be more obedient so that you'll be setting a better example.

- Make your group's goals specific, too.

- Write your goals down. Keep them in mind. Remember the swimmer who wanted to beat fifty-five seconds in the 100-meter freestyle. She wrote F-I-F-T-Y F-I-V-E-! across her fingernails for a month!

5

FLYING TO PUEBLO
The Importance of
Planning

When I was in school, I used to wonder when I was ever going to need all those weird math formulas I had to learn. Well, I knew now as I filled up my second page of calculations. I was filling out a navigation log for a flight from Salt Lake City to Pueblo, Colorado. Because I had never been to Pueblo, I knew I wouldn't be able to fly just by looking down at the ground as I often did. Instead, I would be relying on my instruments and planning.

I was surprised at how much math it took, but by the time I was finished, I had my flight planned to the smallest detail. I knew how to correct for the wind. I knew how much fuel I'd need. I knew what turns I'd have to make to avoid certain dangers and when to make them. I knew how high I'd need to fly. I knew what radio frequencies I'd need to monitor, and I had them written down. I knew how long the flight would take, and I knew what time I'd be landing.

Does that sound like a lot of work? It was. By the time I had finished, I almost thought I'd need to buy new batteries for my calculator. But it was all necessary. If I had simply taken off and climbed above the clouds, I would have had no idea when to come back down. For me, getting it all planned out in advance was the most important part of the flight. And so it is with leadership.

You'll find that few skills will help you as a leader as much as the ability to plan. When you learn to plan well, many other leadership skills will simply fall into place. You'll be able to work around your group's needs. You'll find it easier to control the group. You'll be able to make use of your evaluations.

During a youth conference, a group of young people was divided into smaller groups of ten that were asked to form human pyramids. "Start with four people on the bottom," their leader said, "then three, then two, then one on top."

In an instant, everyone was piling on top of one another, much the way college cheerleaders do at ball games. The problem was, not many of the kids really had any idea of how to make a good pyramid. People came tumbling down even before anyone got all the way to the top.

One team, though, tried something different. Instead of bursting right into the activity, the team members took a few minutes to think it through. And they suddenly realized that no one had ever said they actually had to climb *on* one another. So, finding a clear spot of grass, they simply lay down in formation to make a perfect 4–3–2–1 pyramid which won the contest.

As much fun as it is to jump right into an activity, that's usually not the best approach. More often some good, thoughtful planning is necessary to achieve a quick, efficient solution.

A photographer I once worked with told me how a magazine asked him to fly from Salt Lake City to Mt. Hood,

Oregon, to photograph a member of the United States ski team.

"He'll be in Mt. Hood tomorrow," his editor said. "He's flying out from Park City tonight, so you should be able to reach him anytime tomorrow."

The photographer suddenly cut in. "You mean he's in Park City right now? Park City, *Utah?*"

"That's right. He's been racing there all day."

Park City was only an hour's drive from my friend's home. Had anyone thought out the assignment carefully in advance, my friend could have made the short drive to Park City, shot the story, and been finished. As it was, he had to buy round-trip airfare to Oregon. He had to spend several nights in an expensive lodge. His bill came to more than a thousand dollars in expenses alone. With a little planning, the whole thing could have been done with a twenty-five-dollar trip to Park City.

Actually, planning is a simple process. All it takes is a little time and a lot of thought. When you begin planning your group's next project, just follow these steps:

First, consider the task. Be sure you know what it is you want to have done. Write down the goals you want to achieve.

Second, list your resources. Decide how each person in the group will be able to help. Find ways for every person to contribute in the way he or she does best. And don't forget about physical resources. Do you know anyone who can get you the paint you need? Do you know anyone with a video recorder? Make a list of the things you'll need, and write down the names of the people who can help you get them.

Third, organize your plan. Write it on paper. Outline the steps you'll need to follow, and place them in the order you need to do them. Next to each step, list assignments for each person. As you do that, be sure to consider alternatives. If there is a better, quicker, easier way to get the job done, do it. And learn to assign your physical needs logically. If someone's father owns a hardware store, put that person in charge of getting the paint and brushes.

While you're organizing your plan, don't be afraid to ask for help. Let the group help out. Brainstorm if you need to. The more people you have working on the problem, the better the chance of finding a solution.

When I was in high school, some friends and I spent part of our summer vacation backpacking through New Mexico. None of us had ever been there before, but we didn't worry about that. We had a good map, and we planned our route carefully. Before we set out, we knew exactly where we were going. We knew what mountains we were going to climb. We knew what trails we were going to follow.

Matt, one of my best friends, went a step further. He planned each of our meals, deciding what we were going to eat and when we were going to eat it. I was always glad he did because he saved us a lot of weight.

Instead of just packing a sack of mix for our pancakes, Matt took the time to figure out exactly how much mix he would need to make five pancakes for each person. Then he measured that amount of mix and placed it in a plastic bag that he labeled, "Friday's breakfast." He did the same thing with each meal so that we weren't packing any more food than we really needed. It was a lot of work, but fifteen miles down the trail we were all thanking him for the weight he saved us.

One of the best planners I know is a sixteen-year-old gymnast named Tami. When preparing a floor exercise— her best event—she first decides which stunts she will perform. She knows the requirements (one easy trick, four intermediate tricks, one difficult trick, and as many others as she can fit into a seventy-five-second routine), and she knows her own limitations. She's realistic about her abilities, and she plans her routines accordingly.

Tami also plans a lot of cleverness into her act. She doesn't have good leaps — which are a required part of her routine — so she plans her routines so that she does her leaps at the far end of the mat where the judges can't see them quite so easily. At state meets — where judges are positioned at all four corners — she plans her weakest skills for the center of the mat. She plans her strongest tricks, on the other hand, so they appear where the judges will have the best look at them.

That's creative!

To plan a job well, you've got to think your problems out in advance too, and find answers to them ahead of time. That means having a few emergency plans available in case things don't go the way you expect them to.

I was flying cross-country one time when a red light suddenly began flashing on the instrument panel. It meant that I was losing voltage.

Now, I had always thought I was a good pilot. I had studied everything I could about the planes I flew. And though I recalled reading the steps for dealing with low voltage, I couldn't remember them now.

So reaching beneath my seat, I fished out my pilot's checklist. I quickly flipped through the pages — passing up steps for dealing with fires in flight, electrical problems, icing, power loss, and engine problems. Then, suddenly, there it was. The procedures for low voltage!

As it turned out, solving the problem was easy:

1. Turn the master switch OFF (both sides).
2. Turn the master switch ON.
3. The low voltage light should blink OFF.

The sheet said that if cycling the switch off and on didn't turn off the light, then the plane should be landed as soon as possible. But that wasn't necessary. I cycled the switch once — and the light blinked off.

I later learned that I never was in much danger. If I had lost voltage, I would have lost the use of my flaps and radios. But the plane would have continued to fly. Even so, I was happy that someone had thought the problem out in advance and had a solution planned for me.

A cross-country skier named Jarom was once touring through the mountains of northern Utah. He was several miles from the nearest road when he suddenly lost control on a steep hill. He pitched face first down the slope and rolled for several feet.

Jarom wasn't hurt by the fall, but one of his skis was. The tip had snapped off about four inches from the top.

If you ski much, then you know that skiing without a tip is nearly impossible. Jarom tried it but wasn't making any progress. He was just beginning to think of the long hike back to the road when one of his friends skied up.

"Here," he said, dropping his pack and fishing something out. "I always carry this with me." With that, he tossed Jarom an emergency ski tip. Jarom fastened it to his broken ski and was able to enjoy the rest of the day.

When we plan activities, we don't like to think of problems we might have to face, but they do happen. It's best to be ready for them so that they don't take you by surprise. Plan for every possible disaster and find solutions for each one. With luck, you'll never need them. But if you do, you'll be glad you have them.

Things to Do Now!

- Consider the next job you have lined up. Think it through before you start. Decide to do it better than it's ever been done before.

- Plan ways to involve everyone in the group. Assign jobs according to each person's needs and abilities.

- Learn to organize yourself. Start carrying a notebook and pencil. Know what you're doing, where you're going, and what's next on the agenda.

- Look for different ways of getting the job done. That doesn't mean to sacrifice quality. But if there's a better, easier way to do it, do it!

6

ANYONE TIE A TIMBERHITCH?

Knowing and Using Resources

The Scoutmaster handed each of the seven boys a length of rope. "Okay," he said. "Anyone know how to tie a one-handed bowline?"

A thirteen-year-old Scout named Bryan raised his hand. "I do."

"Good. Would you please show everyone?"

Bryan stood and passed the rope around his waist. "All right. First, you put the rope around your back and hold it like this." He waited until everyone was ready, then took them step by step through the process of tying the one-handed bowline until everyone could do it.

This was a training and planning conference being conducted by a local Boy Scout troop. All of the troop's officers were there to plan for the coming year and to receive leadership training. Bart Peck, the senior patrol leader, conducted the conference, and his Scoutmaster handled the training sessions.

The Scoutmaster was a genius at this sort of thing. As he watched Bryan teach the one-handed bowline, he nodded his approval, then said, "Good. Now, everyone tie a timberhitch." He looked around. "Anyone not know how to tie a timberhitch?"

Two boys raised their hands. The Scoutmaster turned to a boy named Chris, who had already knotted a timberhitch over the arm of his chair.

"Chris, would you help Mike and Jason?"

"Sure."

After the timberhitch came the clove hitch, sheet bend, two half hitches, water knot, and the figure eight knot. In each instance, the Scoutmaster had Scouts who knew the knots teach those who didn't. Finally, when all of the knots had been covered, the Scoutmaster stepped back and clasped his hands behind his back. He rocked back and forth on his heels.

"How many of you learned new knots just now?" he asked. Every one of the boys raised his hand. "And how many of those knots do you think I know?"

Mike was quick. "All of them." There were various nods of agreement.

The Scoutmaster cocked an eyebrow. "Hold on," he said. "Think about it. Did you actually see me tie any knots?"

"No."

The Scoutmaster spread his hands. "Is it possible, then, that I don't know how to tie any of them?"

There was a thoughtful pause. "Yeah."

"Well, if I didn't teach them to you, who did?"

"We did."

The Scoutmaster jumped forward and slammed his fist down on the table with enough force that water sloshed out of a glass resting more than a foot away. The boys all jumped in surprise. The Scoutmaster's voice surged with enthusiasm.

"Who did?"

Everyone shouted. "We did!"

Suddenly calm again, the Scoutmaster stepped back and pushed his hands deep into his pockets. "You know," he said, "you don't need to know everything to be a good leader. Not if you know how to use your resources."

He paused and met each of the boy's eyes in turn. His voice was low. "Remember that when you're leading your patrols."

The Scoutmaster understood an important principle of leadership: he knew how to use his resources. I'm sure that he knew each of the knots he used that day, but rather than teach them himself, he kept his Scouts busy and involved by having them teach one another. By doing this he also helped them to feel part of the group.

Just as important, the Scoutmaster demonstrated the truth of his statement: "You *don't* need to know everything to be a good leader." A good leader, after all, is not one who knows everything; a good leader is one who is able to draw upon the skills and talents of the group he leads.

I have a friend named Hal who coaches tennis at a junior high school. He didn't start out coaching tennis, but when the former coach moved to another school, Hal was asked to take his place.

Now, Hal knew very little about coaching tennis. He played once in a while, though he was far from being an expert. But Hal *was* a leader. The first thing he did was talk to each of the boys on the team. He found out which players had the best serves and which had the best footwork. It turned out that while Hal had only one or two players he considered stars, nearly everyone had strengths in some aspect of the game.

As practice began, Hal paired his players according to their needs. Players who served well taught those who needed help. Players who were good at the net helped those who were less aggressive. Not only were the boys improving their tennis skills, but they were helping to teach others. Everyone felt needed and important. Even though Hal knew only the basics of the sport, by using his resources he was able to develop a team that competed well throughout the year.

One problem faced by many leaders is that they don't know the members of the group well enough to know their particular skills and talents. That can happen when a group is just newly formed or when someone takes over an existing group. Often you can let the group function as it is until you have time to learn more about everyone. But sometimes you don't have time.

When I was in college, I used to work as a guide on the Colorado River. For a couple of weeks each summer I guided white-water raft trips down the Grand Canyon, sometimes spending as many as eighteen days at a time shooting rapids. To be certified, I was required to receive training in first aid. So were each of the other guides, though we rarely faced emergencies more dangerous than cut fingers and sunburned legs.

On one trip a partner and I were escorting nine passengers through the Grand Canyon. On our first day out, we were driving the boat through a strip of boiling rapids when a woman was suddenly tossed from position, gashing her leg against a metal rack. My partner quickly steered the boat back into calmer water and took a careful look at the bleeding wound.

"Nothing to worry about," he said, both to his patient and to the other passengers, who had gathered around. "I've been trained in first aid. I'll have this fixed up in a jiffy."

And then, with considerable enthusiasm, he began cleaning the wound, explaining each step of the procedure as he did.

"This is called neosporin," he said at one point, showing a small white bottle to his attentive audience. "When I pour it over the wound, it seeps inside and bubbles dirt and germs back up to the surface."

The passengers ooed and aahed as if viewing some spectacular miracle of science.

After cleaning the wound, he dressed it, instructing his patient on how to care properly for it. "You've got to keep it dry," he cautioned. "If the dressing gets wet, it'll allow germs to move in from the outside and down into the wound."

The patient nodded solemnly, promising to keep the dressing clean and dry.

Later that night, around the evening campfire, we organized an informal introduction session so we could learn more about our passengers. It turned out that of the nine people with us, six — including the patient — were doctors, and the other three were registered nurses.

We laughed about the incident later, but it illustrates a point. My partner was doing a job when there were people on hand far more qualified than he was to do it. In fact, everyone on hand was more qualified than he was to do it.

It doesn't make sense to have someone with little interest in stars teach an astronomy session if someone else can point out Altair, Vega, and Deneb. But when it comes time to assign certain tasks, many leaders don't know who, if anyone, has the needed skill or interest. One way to find out is through a survey. Consider the tasks you have to do, jot down the assignments that need to be made, then take a survey to find out what you need to know. A class president forming a committee, for instance, may need an art director, a publicity chairman, and a finance chairman. Before making these assignments, he might distribute a survey such as this one.

Personal Resource Survey				
Check the box that best applies to you.	Very skilled	Somewhat skilled	Not skilled	Not skilled but would like to learn
Drawing				
Singing				
Painting				
Carpentry				
Writing				
Mathematics				
Acting				
Sports				
Managing				
Musical instruments (which?)				
Leading music				

Favorite hobbies? _____

Favorite school subjects? _____

Just as important as skills, interests, and talents are physical resources. The class president in our example might want to know if anyone has access to paint, party materials, or poster paper.

I remember once hearing of six boys who had become lost while hiking. After wandering through the woods in circles for several hours, one of the younger boys quietly approached the leader of the bunch and handed him a chart.

"Here's a map," he said. "Maybe it will help."

The older boy was furious. "You've got a map? Why didn't you say anything?"

"Because you never asked!"

It may seem silly, but don't wait for people to volunteer their resources. Ask!

A similar incident was reported by United Press International during the winter of 1985. Two fourteen-year-old boys were hiking in the snow-covered mountains east of Salt Lake City when they became trapped on a rocky ledge. Thick fog swirled all around, reducing visibility to zero. The sun was going down. They both knew they would be forced to spend the night.

The boys had plenty of matches, and one of them even happened to be carrying a small survival handbook. As the mountains grew dark and the temperature dropped, the boys worked hard to build a fire. They searched the ledge for dry kindling, and then scoured the rocks for tinder. Unfortunately, the wood was wet and wouldn't light.

The survival manual had plenty of suggestions for getting the fire burning, but nothing seemed to work. The boys read and reread the manual, trying and retrying every suggestion. But still, no fire.

After about two hours — with fingers numb and spirits dampened — the two finally tried one more trick: they burned the book. And within minutes they had a roaring blaze.

"I don't know why we didn't think of it sooner," one said.

When you have a group to lead and a job to do, find

out first what resources you have available. Get to know the members of your team well enough so that when you need to make an assignment, you'll know who is best suited for the job. Learn what physical items the group may be able to contribute. Most important, give each member the chance to contribute in areas of personal strength. Not only will everyone feel a sense of importance, but each person will have the chance to learn, to share, and to grow.

Things to Do Now!

- Jot down the names of the people you lead, and make a list of each person's skills and talents.

- Write down ways to use the talents of each person. Think of ways to keep everyone involved. Give everyone the chance to contribute and feel important.

- If you don't know your group well enough to do that, make a survey. Get to know every person!

7

TWO PLUS TWO IS WHAT?

Effective Communicating

I t was third down and inches. Ahead by a touchdown, Hillcrest had the ball on Myton's forty-eight-yard line. A first down now could give them the field position they needed for a final drive at the goal line and a chance to frost the win.

Quarterback Chris Ellertson crouched in the huddle and carefully repeated the play the high school coach had given him. "Split left, twenty-three dive, two quick out on three. Ready? Break!"

The team clapped hands and jogged back to the line of scrimmage. Crouching behind center, Chris looked left, then right as Myton linebackers suddenly charged the line. They were going to blitz!

Chris knew he had to call a different play. And he knew he didn't have much time. Turning quickly to both sides, he called an audible: "Red right, thirty-one lead! Red right, thirty-one lead!"

Then crouching again behind center he yelled: "Hut one! Hut two! Hut! Hut!"

The center snapped the ball crisply into Chris's hands. Chris turned and ran sharply to the left. With defensive linebackers blitzing from both sides, he wanted to throw a short pass over the top. Unfortunately, he hadn't given the play correctly. Players turned and ran in the wrong direction as opposing linemen poured over the line. Chris turned once, then doubled over as three defensive giants plowed him down, sacking him for a five-yard loss.

Hillcrest managed to hold on to win the game—barely. But Chris's mistake nearly cost his team the game. One little mistake nearly meant the difference between winning and losing. And it was all a matter of communicating.

We've all had times when a mix-up in communications has caused us trouble or embarrassment. And we'll probably have many more. The problem is, we usually don't realize that there's been a mix-up until it's too late. When we give directions to someone else, we know what we want done. We assume the other person understands. And it usually isn't until it's too late that we learn how well our instructions were really understood.

An English teacher I had in high school once told us about a student who became sick midway through the term. The student's mother came to school one day to pick up her daughter's work for the rest of the term. Mrs. Cameron gave her several projects and tests the girl would need to complete.

"I'll let you administer these," Mrs. Cameron said. "Your daughter's a fine young lady, and I don't worry about her cheating."

After several weeks, though, none of the assignments had been returned. The term was nearing its end, and Mrs. Cameron had no choice but to send home a failing notice.

A couple of days later the mother was back in school demanding to know why her daughter was failing.

Mrs. Cameron spread her hands. "Because she hasn't turned in any of the work I sent her!"

The mother blushed. "Oh . . . we didn't know you wanted us to bring it back."

Even the most obvious things are sometimes misunderstood. No matter how clear something may seem, make sure it's understood!

Being able to communicate effectively is a skill that will determine your success as a leader. If you can convey your instructions in a way that everyone understands — and in a way that will spark everyone's enthusiasm — your job will be half done.

How do you do that? Let's look at a couple of ways.

First, before you begin any project, make sure that every person knows what's supposed to happen.

You've probably had times when you've thought, "Nobody ever tells me anything." And you know how frustrating it is when you don't know what's going on. So be open and honest about your plans. Let everyone know what's happening.

I wrote a magazine story about snowmobiling through Yellowstone one winter, and I spent a whole hour one day talking with drivers as they came in to see Old Faithful. One thing they all said was that snowmobiles weren't much fun when someone else was driving.

"It's scary," said a fourteen-year-old boy named Mike. "When you're on the back, you don't have any control. You never know where the driver's going, and you never know what he's going to do next."

Unless you learn to communicate well, the people you lead will often feel like Mike on the back of a snowmobile. It's important that you let everyone know clearly where you're going and what you're doing.

Second, be sure that every person knows exactly what you expect. See that every person knows clearly what his or her duties and responsibilities are. Let each person know what you want him or her to do.

Air traffic controllers know all about this principle. And

they have a neat trick for making sure that pilots know what they're supposed to do after takeoff. After telling them which runway to use, how high to climb, when to turn, and which radio frequency to use, controllers have the pilots *repeat the information.* If the pilot has any trouble remembering—or if he says something wrong—the controller repeats the correct information.

Good idea! See if your followers can repeat *your* instructions back in their own words. If they can't, repeat your instructions again a little more clearly. Remember that good communication is a two-way street and that those you lead are not mind readers.

To do their best work, group members need to know what is expected of each one. They each need to know their specific duties. If you are unable to communicate this information clearly, expect disaster!

A word of warning. Don't think just because you've told everyone what to do that you're finished. As you begin any project, new questions will come up. Someone may run into a problem and not know what to do. New situations will develop.

A ski instructor was once teaching his class of beginning skiers how to get on a chair lift.

"It's easy," he said. "All you have to do is stand on the line. Hold your poles in your left hand, look over your right shoulder, then just sit down when the chair comes up to you. Everybody got it? Good! Let's give it a try!"

Everyone was anxious about the first ride on the chair lift. The instructor stayed close by to help out and encourage the younger ones who were afraid. Everything went fine, and soon everyone was riding the lifts peacefully up the mountain. And then one of the young skiers suddenly realized something. No one had told them how to get off!

As the midway point approached—the spot where the class was supposed to get off—everyone became more and more excited. No one had told them what to do, and there was no one to ask. When they arrived at the midway point, the braver skiers just piled off. But the more timid ones ended up riding clear to the top of the mountain.

The third step, then, is to keep your communication lines open! Talk to the group often about how things are going. Re- emphasize your expectations. Ask for questions. Listen to what's going on.

You should remember that *receiving* information is just as important as giving it. Remember that when you use a telephone, you need to use the receiver as much as the mouthpiece. When you talk to the group, be certain you're tuned in to them. Find out how they feel about what's happening. Make sure you understand their feelings.

A high school tennis coach was once preparing her team for a tournament. She knew the competition would be tough, so she pushed her team hard. Probably a little too hard. The endless workouts were beginning to take their toll. Many of the players were becoming discouraged.

Finally, when the coach ordered the team back to the courts for another workout, she heard a player named Jan say, "Well, here we go again—back to the pits."

Now, Jan was one of the team's best players. She rarely complained. So when the coach heard her murmuring, she knew that Jan was unhappy. For the first time she realized that maybe she was working everyone a little too hard.

"Tell you what," she said, changing her mind. "Let's all hit the showers. Then let's go out for a pizza!"

The team came instantly back to life.

"All right!" everyone chorused.

This coach was tuned in to her team. She was used to hearing players complain. Yet she was sensitive enough to know the difference between idle chatter and discouragement. So must you be.

While we're talking about receiving, don't underestimate your resources. If you listen carefully to what the group is saying, you may come up with a new idea or two. Maybe you'll even come up with a *better* idea. (Two—or more—heads are better than one, remember?) And even if you don't, something that someone says may prompt *you* to come up with a better idea.

You'll be surprised at this. But people will flood you with ideas if you give them a chance and they know that you'll listen. Next time you find yourself stumped for an idea, just try listening to what everyone else is thinking.

Things to Do Now!

- Speak clearly when talking or giving instructions. Remember to speak loudly enough for everyone to hear. Speak slowly enough for those who might be taking notes.

- Learn to look at people when you talk with them. If they begin squirming as you give them instructions, there's a chance that they don't understand what you're asking of them. And if they're not looking back at you, maybe they're not even listening.

- Learn to look at people when they're talking with you. A person may tell you that John's doing a great job, but his eyes might tell you differently.

- The next time you give instructions, see if they can repeat the information back in their own words. Make sure they understand what you want.

- Learn to summarize. After you've given a lesson—or after you've explained something—repeat the whole idea in a few short words. Better to sound like a broken record than face a mix-up.

8

How to Catch a Fish

*Controlling the
Group*

Tyson Cayley waded knee-deep in the water and cast his hook toward the middle of the lake. He held his pole even with the surface and let the line run loosely through his left hand.

After a moment he felt a tug on the line. A second later he felt it again. He set the hook and began reeling furiously.

"Yahoo!" he shouted. "I've got another one! A monster!"

Roger Pace, standing just a few feet away, looked over in disbelief.

"You've got *another* one? I can't believe it!"

Tyson's pole was bent at a crazy angle — his line slicing through the water — as he reeled.

"Yeah! And it's a monster!"

Roger glanced once toward his own bobber — which was floating lazily on the lake as it had all morning — then sighed and placed his pole in the fork of a stick.

"I can't believe it," he said. "I'm standing less than ten feet from you, and I haven't had a bite all day."

"And this is my fifth fish!" Tyson shouted.

Roger reached for his net and waded over to Tyson's side.

"Almost got 'im," Tyson said. There was an arc of silver as the fish flashed through the water.

Roger whisked the net over the water, then sent it plunging beneath the surface. A moment later he pulled the fat trout from the water. He shook his head.

"Okay," he said. "I give up. I want to try some of those grasshoppers you're using."

Grasshoppers? That's all it had taken for Tyson to catch five fish. It may not sound like a big deal, but standing just a few feet away, baiting his hook with marshmallows, Roger hadn't caught a thing all morning.

I have a friend named Sam who had an experience much like Tyson and Roger's. He was ice fishing on Scofield Reservoir. Like everyone else he drilled a small hole in the ice, dropped his line until it touched bottom, then raised it about six inches. Right away he began catching fish. So was nearly everyone else.

Not too far way was a young man who wasn't having any luck. Standing near his hole with his hands in his pockets he watched as people all around him caught fish. Finally, when he couldn't stand it anymore, he decided to change bait. Since he didn't have anything but cheese, he asked another fisherman if he could borrow a few salmon eggs. And a couple of minutes later he had his first fish.

If you've ever been fishing, then you know that you can't force a fish to take your hook. But if you offer it the right bait you can probably convince it to at least take a couple of nibbles.

Controlling a group is often like that. You can't force people to behave. And you can't force them to do the things you want them to. But with the right incentives you can entice them a little.

I once had a science teacher who knew that. And he used it to control his classes.

"I'd like you to answer the questions on page 143," he'd tell us. "And I'll give bonus points for every problem you have done by the end of class."

With that he'd leave us to it. He never had to shout to keep us quiet, and he never had to get mad at us. We were too busy being good — we were too busy doing our work! — to have time to be noisy. And if someone in the room wasn't interested in the bonus points — well, that someone had a hard time finding anyone to talk to!

One of my neighbors works at a fast food store. She learned some good lessons about controlling from her shift boss.

"We used to be really bad," Andrea told me. "During rush hours the work was always hard and tiring. And when things slowed down, it got boring. Most of us hated work."

Andrea's boss tried her best to boost morale but never could. And so her employees were lazy and discouraged, and their service lacked quality.

After a number of weeks a new manager took over. And right away she began changing things. Just before rush hour one day she said, "I'll give a $5 bonus to the waitress who serves the most customers in the next hour."

For the first time in weeks everyone in the store was looking for someone to help.

"May I help you?" one would say as soon as she had completed an order.

"Is there *anyone* who isn't being helped," pleaded another from the side.

The service might have lacked sincerity at first, but it was a start. With a small incentive, attitudes had changed. The new boss could have improved performance by getting mad, yelling, and maybe even firing a few people. But she didn't. Instead, she found ways to reward those who worked the way she wanted them to. She made them *want* to work hard.

There's a good lesson in that. After all, it shouldn't be the fear of punishment that keeps people in line. It should be the fear of missing out on something good.

During a Boy Scout camp out, a patrol leader named Wyatt needed to have his patrol clean up the many small pieces of garbage that littered the campsite.

"There's a certain piece of garbage out there," he told everyone. "And I'll give a candy bar to the person who finds it."

In an instant the boys were out scouring the campsite. They weren't working for fear of being punished; they were working for fear of missing out!

I once had an English teacher who used similar tactics to get her English classes to listen to her lessons.

"I'm going to write five words on the blackboard," she said. "And I'll use each of those words in my lesson today. Listen for each one and write it down when you hear it. For everyone who can list the words in the order I use them, I'll award five bonus points."

Five bonus points weren't much, but many of us needed every point we could get! And you can bet we were all listening hard as she presented her lesson that day.

When it comes to discipline and control, preventing problems is far better than facing them head on. If you can find ways to make the group members want to work, your job will be easier to do. If you can find ways to make them *want* to behave, they'll be good even when you're not around to keep an eye on them.

Of course, you can't really expect to lead without meeting someone who doesn't act up once in a while. And how you deal with that is very important. If you holler, shout, or lose control, you might also lose the respect of those you lead. And you'll probably just make the situation worse. But if you can react to the situation calmly, you'll keep everyone's temper cool. You'll be able to handle the situation much more effectively.

During a high school basketball game, a key player named Dan got into a fight with an opposing player. Both players were ejected immediately from the game.

Dan's coach was mad as a hornet. After all, the team was behind, and they *needed* Dan. But rather than chasing him down and yelling at him, the coach gave himself time to cool down. Then after the game he took Dan aside for a talk.

"What happened out there?" he asked.

Dan shook his head angrily. "The guy kept pushing me!" he said. "He kept jabbing me with his elbows!"

The coach nodded. "So what did you do?"

Dan made a fist. "Finally I just lost my temper and belted him."

"Did that solve the problem?"

"No. I guess not. I ended up hurting the team."

"What do you think that you *should* have done?"

"I should have talked to the ref. Or to you. I know I shouldn't have blown up like that."

Dan knew he had made a dumb mistake. He knew it the minute he threw the first punch. And if his coach had gone storming into the locker room yelling about how Dan nearly cost his team the whole game, he wouldn't have been telling Dan anything that he didn't already know.

Instead, the coach gave himself and Dan some time to cool down. He let Dan analyze his own actions. There was no way he could have gotten Dan back into the ball game. But by handling the situation the way he did, he made sure that Dan understood the seriousness of his actions. He made sure that Dan would remember the lesson the next time.

Try this the next time you get mad. Give yourself a little time to cool down, then take the person you're mad at aside for a little talk. Remember that he probably knows what he's done wrong. So rather than point it out to him, let *him* analyze his actions. This will help him to understand the mistake he's made.

It also helps if you have a few clear, specific consequences outlined just in case. Make sure everyone knows
what they are. And make sure everyone knows that if
someone chooses to act wrongly, that person also chooses
to accept the consequence.

I used to work at an aquatics base where we taught
boating, skiing, sailing, and snorkeling. The days were
warm, but the nights were exceptionally cold, and no one
ever wanted to get out of bed in the mornings. Our pro-
gram director, though, insisted on having a staff meeting
at seven o'clock each morning down by the lake. He never
ordered anyone to be there. But he made it clear that anyone who didn't show up—and anyone who was late—
would be assigned K.P. for the entire day.

No one ever got yelled at for being late. No one ever
got mad. But they all knew that if they were late, they
were on K.P. that day. It was a fair rule, and it was fair
discipline. No one could complain when they found their
name on the K.P. roster.

It also helps if you remember that people always have
reasons for the way they act. If you come to know the people
you lead and understand why they do what they do, you'll
be in a far better position for discipline.

And when they come to know that you really care about
them, they'll respond better. If they make a mistake, show
them that you're worried about *them* first, and the *job* second. It's tough to do, sometimes. Especially if you're just
getting started with the group. But if you're consistent and
fair, the group will learn to respond.

Your best bet is to keep the group members busy and
active. Keep them moving in a positive direction, and reward them for their good efforts. If you keep them busy
enough, they won't have time to get into mischief. And if
they do, have a few consequences ready. They don't need
to be tough ones. The simple fact that you have them is
often enough to get the message across.

Things to Do Now!

• Find ways to reward those who behave the way you want them to. A simple, "Good job!" is often all it takes.

• Make certain that everyone knows your expectations. You can't expect group members to sit quietly unless they know that's what you expect them to do.

• Be fair and consistent. Treat everyone in the group equally. It's easy to play favorites, but it's important that you don't!

• Have a couple of consequences ready just in case. Remember that these really don't need to be harsh. Often just the fact that you have them is enough.

9

HAMBURGERS, EGGS, AND BANANA BOATS
Effective Teaching

Now this is the way to cook hamburger!" Erika Morrey stepped away from the campfire and molded a ball of hamburger into an empty orange peel. She trimmed away a bit of extra meat and then carefully set the orange peel into a bed of glowing coals.

"Ummm, she said, wiping her hands clean on her chef's apron. "Can't you just taste it?"

The nine girls standing around the campfire nodded eagerly. Their mouths were already watering.

"You see, by cooking your meat in the orange, you don't have any pans to clean," Erika explained. "And the orange peel gives the hamburger a special flavor you just can't get at the Burger Palace!"

Erika smiled. Her fire, shaped like a keyhole and lined with rocks, blazed cheerfully. Off to one side was a platform made of dry pine branches and loaded with firewood.

A couple of feet away was another platform made of branches, this one about three feet off the ground and covered with food.

Erika was teaching a lesson on primitive cooking. And she held her fifteen-year-old students spellbound as she taught them.

"You might have noticed the way I've shaped my fire," she said as she began molding another hamburger patty. "It's shaped like a keyhole for a very important reason. I can keep the fire burning up here at the top, and I can scrape the coals down into the narrow part to cook over. That way I can have flames and coals at the same time."

Erika took her hamburger patty and slapped it onto the side of a flat rock facing the coals.

"There. Flat rocks make great barbeques when you can't find an orange peel."

Erika's next trick was to boil an egg in a paper cup. Really! Taking an ordinary unwaxed cup, she filled it with water, plopped the egg into it, and set it right in the middle of the hottest coals. The rim of the cup quickly burned away, but the rest of it remained unharmed.

And that wasn't all. She cooked bacon and eggs in the bottom of a paper bag, heated a banana stuffed with chocolate chips and marshmallows, and baked a "cake" in another orange peel.

You've probably seen people do primitive cooking lessons before. So have I. But they have never been taught as cleverly as Erika's lesson. Trying to make the experience as realistic as possible, she even had her girls follow a quarter-mile compass course through the woods to find her backcountry kitchen.

Erika was a master teacher. She knew how to take a topic and squeeze out every bit of fun there was in it. She did it with primitive cooking, she did it with sewing, and she did it with spiritual topics, too. Her lessons were always fun, and they were always remembered.

I'm sure you know teachers like Erika. They love the subjects they teach, and they go to great lengths to teach them well. They don't just make them fun—they make them meaningful.

A Scout leader named Travis once took a group of boys deep into the mountains of southern Utah. For three days they camped and hiked, and soon everyone was covered with thick layers of dirt. Travis decided they all needed a lesson on how to keep clean in the mountains, but instead of just giving the boys a stiff lecture, Travis called them all together one night after dinner.

"Everyone tired?" he asked as the boys took seats around the blazing bonfire he had built.

The boys nodded.

"Me, too," Travis said. "So I thought we could all just sit here for a few minutes and talk."

With that, Travis began telling stories. Mostly about mountainmen, Indians, grizzly bears, and other things that boys find interesting. After a few minutes, without breaking the rhythm of his story, he unbuttoned his dusty shirt, removed it, and folded it over a nearby pine branch.

"There was a trapper who once had to run his horse 125 miles with a band of mad Indians hot on his tail the whole way," Travis said as if he were doing nothing unusual. "He'd spur his horse until he had a two- or three-hundred-yard lead, then he'd slow down to rest and take off when the Indians started getting close again."

As he talked, he pulled a bandanna from his pocket and poured a little water from his canteen over it. Still telling his story, he used the bandanna as a washcloth and began washing his face and arms.

After a moment—in the middle of a story about John Wesley Powell now—he unlaced his boots. He paused long enough to make a point and then removed his boots and socks and washed his feet.

The boys watched all this with wide eyes. Many of

them were even rubbing their dirt-caked arms and legs, longing to be a shade cleaner themselves.

Finally Travis toweled himself dry, pulled on a fresh shirt and clean socks, and laced up his boots. He smiled, clapped his hands, and said good night.

Not once did Travis say a word about staying clean. Not once did he say anything about taking baths. But so well did he teach his lesson that every boy had taken a backcountry bath that night before going to bed.

With a little creativity, you can teach many important lessons, too. You can make your lessons meaningful. The key is to find ways to get everyone to *want* to learn.When you are called upon to teach—when your group needs training or instruction—find ways to let everyone know that the things you're teaching them are important. Convince them that the skills they are learning are useful. Let them see that your motive is to help *them*.

Many teachers find success by emphasizing performance. They make certain their students have the opportunity to use the things they learn. Drama instructors, for instance, produce plays. English teachers publish newspapers and magazines. Coaches organize games and contests.

When I was in junior high, I had a friend named Burke who played the trumpet. He liked playing in the band, and he was good at it. But he never practiced as hard as he did when he had a big solo coming up in a concert. Most people are like that.

So if you're going to teach cooking, make certain you give everyone the opportunity to cook! (Better yet, let the class know that someone is going to *eat* the things they cook!) If you're going to teach knot tying and lashing, find something for them to build!

I once attended a citizen's academy taught by the Orem, Utah, police department. Once a week we learned about patrol tactics, crime investigation, firefighting, and other aspects of police work. All of our instructors were performance oriented. After a lesson on search procedures, we were marched to a nearby building and told there was a burglar inside. We were each given pistols (loaded with blanks) and flashlights and told to search the building.

Even though I knew it was a game, the experience was so real my palms were sweating as I searched.

Later we learned about accident investigation. After the lesson, we were taken to a nearby street where a typical accident had been staged. We had to study the scene and decide which car had caused the accident.

We all knew it wasn't real. But during class we *knew* we would be making searches. We *knew* we would be investigating accidents. So we listened *hard* to what we were being taught.

Many times this success formula can also be used in reverse. Instead of teaching a skill and promising an opportunity to do it later, many teachers expose their students to a problem and let them see how frustrating it can be. Then the students are prepared when the teacher asks, "Now, would you like to see an easier way?"

A college math professor once gave some difficult problems to a class I was in. After letting us struggle with them for several minutes, he asked, "How's it going?"

When most of us grumbled that things weren't going very well at all, he asked, "Would any of you be interested in learning a shortcut?"

You bet we were! And every eye in the room was on the blackboard as he demonstrated a simple solution for difficult problems. By exposing us to the problem ahead of time, our teacher neatly prepared us for his lesson. He let us see a need for a better way. And by the time he was ready to teach it, we were ready—and eager—to learn it.

I once saw a recreation teacher do that. He had his backpacking students come to class with fully loaded backpacks—some of them weighing thirty or forty pounds—

and had them march a full mile around the college campus. By the time they returned to class, the young backpackers knew how miserable a heavy pack could be. And they were ready when their instructor showed them how to load a pack so it was easiest to carry.

This formula is effective for three reasons. It lets everyone see exactly how much he or she knows about what's going on. It convinces them all that they would benefit by knowing more. And it gives them a desire to know more. Once they have that desire, they'll be *asking* for more!

You'll find that people learn best those things they want to learn. They learn best when they have a compelling reason for learning. So your challenge is to take the things you want to teach and find ways to get your students to want to learn.

A young woman named Vicki told me about a home economics class she had in high school. The class was once scheduled to learn about hazards in the kitchen—something most girls thought would be rather boring.But when they arrived in the classroom, the teacher had arranged the kitchen in careful disorder. A can of cleanser was placed near the flour bin. An electric cord from the toaster trailed through the sink. Knives in the drainer were placed blade up.

Rather than giving a lecture, the teacher challenged her students to find as many hazards as they could. Students were given points for finding hazards, and they were given points for explaining why the situation was dangerous.

With a little imagination and creativity, the teacher had taken a dull topic and made an enjoyable — and valuable — lesson out of it.

During a district camporee, a Scoutmaster found a way to give his troop some practice in knots and lashings. (And if you're a Boy Scout, you probably know how dull that can be!) But this Scoutmaster was an inspired teacher, and he had a few tricks up his sleeve.

Assembling his boys near the edge of the river, he held out a bowl containing gingerbread men decorated as Scouts.

"My wife made these," he said. "And I'm going to give them to Troop 870."

The boys howled in protest. Troop 870 was their arch rival. For the Scoutmaster to give presents to the enemy troop rankled even the most easygoing boys in the troop.

"You can't do that!" one protested.

"Well, I'm sorry," the Scoutmaster said. "But I didn't realize that you'd want them so badly." He motioned toward a pile of ropes and pioneering poles that had been set out along the river bank. "Of course, there might be a way out."

The boys were instantly enthusiastic. "What is it?"

"Well, I told them to come for the gingerbread men at noon. It's now 10:45. If you could build a bridge and get everyone across the river by noon, I suppose there wouldn't be any way we could share them."

Bart, the senior patrol leader, jumped forward. "Yeah! Let's do it!"

"There is just one more thing," the Scoutmaster said. "To be fair, I'm going to let the Scoutmaster of Troop 870 inspect the bridge before I let anyone cross. If it's not put together correctly — if the knots and lashings aren't all tied the way they should be — I won't let anyone across. Fair enough?"

That was more than fair. And an instant later the boys were busy lashing poles, pounding stakes, and tying knots, knowing they were working under a fierce deadline. And they made it, too — barely. More important, they had been given a good reason — a good incentive — for practicing dull skills and for doing top-quality work.

When it is your turn to teach an important skill or concept, be sure your students have ample incentive to learn it. Give them opportunities to perform the things they've learned. Show them the importance of what you're teaching them. Once the group has seen that your lessons are going to benefit *them*, your lessons will come alive. You'll find the group eager to learn and hungry for more. And you'll find them ready for the many other important lessons you have for them.

Things to Do Now!

- Vow that you'll never — ever — read your lessons straight from the lesson manual!

- Begin planning your next lesson right now. Give yourself plenty of time (at least a week whenever you can). Give it plenty of thought. Find ways to relate it to the lives of those you're teaching.

- Find some way to make your next lesson come alive. Through a demonstration, activity, or discussion, create interest in what you have to teach.

10

DOING THE FLOOR EXERCISE
The Power of
Example

Welcome to Kyoto!"

Elder Hadley shook my hand eagerly and then reached for my suitcase. "Here, let me help you with that."

I smiled gratefully as I buttoned up my coat against the cold Japanese air. "Thanks. I feel like I've been packing it for hours."

"I know," Elder Hadley said. "I had to take three different trains when I transferred here. I didn't think I was ever going to make it."

My new companion led me out of the train station and strapped my suitcase to the back of his own bicycle. "Have you ever been to Kyoto before?"

I shook my head. "First time," I said. "I've been to Himeji a couple of times, but this is my first trip north."

"You'll love it," Elder Hadley assured me. "The people here are terrific. We've got a great ward, and the members really go out of their way to make investigators feel welcome. Just last month we had three baptisms and . . ."

I laughed as I listened to my new companion talk. He spoke with a delightful accent, pronouncing "I" as "Ah" and saying "are" as "or." It was exactly the way one of my favorite companions — a missionary I had worked with several months before — talked. So when Elder Hadley quit talking for a moment I asked, "Do you know Elder Burton?"

"Paul Burton? From Colorado?"

"Yeah — that's the one."

"He was my last companion! We were together for two months!"

I laughed again, no longer surprised. Elder Burton was a fantastic missionary, and after two months with him it was no wonder that even his style of speech had rubbed off on Elder Hadley.

As I spent more time with Elder Hadley I saw that many more of Elder Burton's peculiar habits had rubbed off. My new companion, for instance, began every morning with a series of one-armed push-ups, thirty or so sit-ups, and then more push-ups — something Elder Burton did every morning. Elder Hadley also had the habit of bearing his testimony at every door we visited, something I had never seen anyone but Elder Burton do.

One time I even noticed that Elder Hadley marked his scriptures in the same peculiar way I did. I thought that was unusual until I realized that we had both learned our method from Elder Burton!

Elder Hadley had had no intention of patterning himself after Elder Burton, but example is such a powerful tool that he was influenced by it without even knowing it. Living side by side with Elder Burton for two months made it inevitable that certain traits would rub off.

How glad I was that they were all good traits!

As a leader, you too will influence many people through your example. Those you lead will do the things they see you do. If you are cheerful when the task is hard, many others will be also. If you are obedient, those you lead will be obedient. If you show respect for other people, so will everyone else. Demonstrate through your example how to work hard, how to smile, and how to be obedient, and others will follow. You will never teach leadership as powerfully as you will through the strength of your own example.

I have a friend named Jim who conducts rock climbing courses. He spends much of his time with his students out on the rocks climbing and rappeling. But he also insists that his students learn many other things, including knots. Many of his student climbers can tie the figure-eight knots and bowlines that are so important in rock climbing. But many of them also want to learn such things as the Prusik knot.

The Prusik knot is used for climbing ropes (James Bond uses it all the time). It's one of the easiest knots in the world to tie, but it's almost impossible to describe.

One time Jim was struggling to teach the Prusik to a handful of young climbers. He tried several times to explain what to do, but wasn't making any headway. Finally he gave up and said, "Everybody come here and watch this." He then demonstrated the knot one time. But it was so easy to tie that one time was enough. After just that one demonstration, all the students were able to tie it themselves.

How you lead the Laurels class will depend largely upon how you've seen others do it. More important, future leaders will do it the way they've seen you do it. Many people will pattern themselves after you. If you work hard—if you complete your duties completely and responsibly—there is every chance that others who see you will do the same.

As a leader you might spend a lot of time teaching your followers to work hard, to be honest, and to be cheerful. But not until they see you working hard, being honest, and being cheerful will they get the message. You may tell them to be on time to meetings. But if you're late yourself, forget it.

I have a young cousin who lives for gymnastics. Just twelve years old, Holly has won many junior tournaments. Her coach says that Holly has natural instincts. But Holly says her success comes from watching another gymnast on the team.

"Lorraine does the most beautiful floor exercise I've ever seen," Holly told me. "I could sit and watch her for hours."

Lorraine *was* a fine gymnast. She displayed elegant split leaps and dazzling pirouettes. She executed neat front and back walkovers, and she did graceful full and double toe turns. She was an athlete worthy of imitation.

But Holly did more than just admire her. Every time she watched Lorraine perform, she picked out one move or trick she liked, then tried to do it herself. Sometimes she'd pick an easy skill that came quickly. And sometimes she picked things that took a little more time and practice before she could do them.

"I learned almost everything I know about the floor exercise from watching Lorraine," Holly said. "Almost all of my tricks are ones that I saw Lorraine do first."

Besides being a good athlete, Lorraine had other skills, too. She knew how to play to an audience. She knew how to smile in a way that didn't seem faked. She made her entrances in a way that seemed to say: "Hey, world! Watch me! I'm having fun!"

Holly was soon doing these same things. No one ever taught her to do them. She learned by watching another gymnast.

You'll find this principle to be true in almost every aspect of leadership. Just as people learn physical skills by watching others, they also learn obedience, trust, and faith by watching those who practice these traits.

Show others through your own example how to be obedient, trusting, and faithful. And even in circles where you're not a designated leader, don't be afraid to let your example set you apart. One person setting the proper example can often change a bad experience into a good one.

A young woman once shared with me an experience she had had at girls' camp. After a long day, several of the campers had gathered and were discussing their camping partners.

"I can't believe Ruth came again this year," one said. "She doesn't do anything but cause trouble."

"Collette's the same way," someone else added. "I wish they'd both just go home."

"They're both spoiled brats," someone else said.

As this was going on, another young woman named Mary became uncomfortable. She didn't like the direction the conversation was taking. And when the campers were about to vote on who they thought was the most spoiled person at camp that year, Mary suddenly said, "Hey! What if we voted on the girl who is the most fun at camp this year? And maybe we could give her an award or something."

The idea was greeted with instant enthusiasm.

"And we could vote on the most spiritual girl, too!" someone else suggested.

"And the most inspiring!"

"And the best dressed!"

At the last suggestion everyone laughed. But as the conversation changed, so did the mood. While many of the girls had been on the verge of anger, now they were laughing as they began preparing awards for campers who were making the camp fun and happy.

Many times you'll be with informal groups, such as this bunch of campers, that do not have leaders. And without someone to keep everyone moving in the right direction, people may unconsciously begin veering the wrong way.

Don't be afraid to give them a nudge back the right direction.

A young neighbor of mine named Doug told me about a time he went camping with the ward Scout troop. As the boys lay in their sleeping bags, an innocent discussion gradually became crude and offensive. Not liking the manner in which the evening was shaping, Doug suddenly called out: "It's 10:30, guys. Why don't we have a minute of silence so everyone can say their prayers?"

The camp was instantly quiet and reverent. And the mood was changed. After a minute or two of silence, the boys gradually began talking again. Many of them talked far into the night, but the conversation never returned to its vulgar beginnings. With a single question — and without any preaching or moralizing — Doug had effectively changed something bad into something good.

A good example can help *you*, too. If you have trouble motivating the group, find someone who's good at motivation and watch him. See how he does it. See if you can learn from his example.

You can learn much about leadership by watching other people lead. You can learn about building character and citizenship by watching others. Watch carefully the things they do. See what things work and what things don't.

In an earlier chapter I mentioned Steve Birrell, the captain of my eighth-grade basketball team. Besides being a good leader, Steve was always happy and full of energy. I wanted to be like him. I wanted people to think of me the way I thought of him.

I didn't want to *be* Steve. I just wanted to be the same sort of person that he was.

So I started doing the sort of things Steve did. Steve often stayed late after practice to pick up towels and store balls in the racks.

I started staying late to help, too.

Whenever Coach Brimhall asked for someone to run

an errand— even if it had nothing to do with basketball—
Steve was always the first to respond.

I started volunteering, too.

One night after practice one of the school custodians
came in to talk with the coach. He said he was cleaning
the auditorium for an activity that night. He wondered if
anyone on the team would be free to help him for a few
minutes.

As usual, Steve's hand shot up. So did mine. And the
two of us spent the next hour picking up paper behind
the bleachers. It wasn't fun work, but we had fun doing
it.

That's the way Steve was. After a game once I saw him
go up and say something to the referees. I'm not sure what
he said, but because both officials smiled, I know it was
something like, "Great game, guys."

After the next game *I* went up and said thanks to the
referees. It took a lot of courage, but I was surprised at
how good it made me feel.

I don't know if anyone ever admired me as much as I
admired Steve. But *I* liked me for the things I was doing.
I knew I was doing good things, and I knew I was improving myself.

Use the power of your own excellent example to shape
those you lead. Demonstrate every day *exactly* the way you
want your followers to behave. Be consistent. Don't worry
if people say you sound like a broken record. *Show* them
what you want of them.

When you begin to look and act like a leader, people
will follow you with confidence. Your example will show
them the way to greatness. Do your best at everything you
do. Have fun while you're at it. And you'll influence many
through your example.

Things to Do Now!

- Think of the example you set for others. Are your actions worthy of being imitated by others? If they're not, improve them!

- Decide what traits you want to see in the people you lead. Do you want them to be honest? Then be honest! Do you want them to be obedient? Then be obedient!

- Find a hero. Or find someone who does things you would like to learn. Learn from his example.

11

GETTING THE COOK STARTED
Applying Leadership

$\mathbf{R}$on Cutler was standing along the Colorado River with his hands in his pockets. One of the best river guides in the Grand Canyon, he was discussing plans for the next day with his boat crews. "We'll need to get an early start on the river tomorrow," he said. "Who's fixing breakfast?"

Todd Nelson lifted a hand. "I am."

"Good. What do we have planned?"

"Hash browns and ham."

"Sounds good. I'm looking forward to that. Can you have them ready by 7:30?"

"No problem."

"Good. Will you need any help?"

"No. I'll be fine."

"Good."

With that, Ron went on to review the next day's schedule and then sent everyone to bed. With a few soft questions and a low-key delivery, he had effectively made certain his crews were ready for another day on the river.

Ron didn't do much yelling as a leader, and he rarely gave orders. He liked to be more subtle. If one of the boats needed a little air, he would wait until one of his crewmen was standing around with nothing to do and then say: "Do you know where the blower is? I think I ought to put a little more air in the boat."

Almost always the crewman would say, "Oh, hey, I'll do that for you."

Ron would look pleased and say, "Why, thanks, Dave. I appreciate that."

And if the cook was late getting dinner started, Ron would start hitching up the butane stoves. He wouldn't actually start cooking, but he'd casually begin making preparations. He rarely spent more than a few minutes doing that before the cook saw him and came running.

"Here, I'll take care of that," he'd say.

And Ron would look pleased again and say, "Thanks, Cam. I appreciate that."

Ron's style of leadership might sound silly, but it was effective. It worked for him because his crew knew what he expected of them. Ron, in turn, knew that his crewmen were capable of doing their jobs. He just kept them moving in the right direction.

Other leaders are sometimes less subtle. As a sportswriter, I used to cover high school football games. I'd stand right on the sidelines where I could walk up and down the field to get the best view of the action. I usually spent half of the game on one side of the field, and I'd switch at halftime. This gave me a better feel for the teams I was covering.

As I did this I was surprised at how different the coaches were. While one stormed the sidelines, shouting and yelling and turning blue in the face, the man across the field might have been pacing quietly back and forth.

I saw coaches who would stomp and yell and throw things (even when their team was winning), and I saw coaches who could watch a player make a spectacular diving catch without showing a trace of excitement.

The interesting thing was that the style of leadership didn't have a whole lot to do with the team's ability to win. Mean coaches won just as often as nice coaches.

You, too, will have your own style of leadership. But you should remember that every person you lead will be different. You have to learn to guide the group according to the needs and abilities of each member. At times you'll want to be forceful. At other times, you'll want to blend a little deeper into the background. Knowing when to hammer in nails with a sledgehammer and when to tap at them gently with your softest mallet will help determine how successful you will be as a leader.

One thing you need to remember is that everyone has different levels of ability. You need to treat people accordingly. Some people, for instance, may be very willing to do what you ask but might not know how. These are people who brim with excitement but don't yet have the proper training.

I have a friend named Norma who is a ski instructor. She likes to tell about a boy named Robert who was in her ski class one year.

"Robert was a natural daredevil," she told me. "He was excited to learn, and he'd try anything."

The trouble was, Robert had never been on skis before in his life. He didn't have any idea how to turn or stop, but that didn't bother him!

Before their first class, Norma spotted Robert bombing down the run, holding his arms out for balance and shouting with excitement. When the run curved, Robert went blasting off into the trees where the soft snow stopped him. Then he picked his way back onto the trail and started over again.

"He was the first skier in the class to parallel," Norma said. "He was so eager to learn I just couldn't hold him back."

People like Robert need opportunities to exercise their enthusiasm. Work with them personally, if you can, until they have the necessary skills to continue on their own. Or place them with someone who knows what to do and who can teach them.

Whatever you do, don't become angry or frustrated with someone if he just doesn't know what to do. Instead, teach him! You'll also meet people who are able to do the job but who don't have the confidence to try. People who are shy may be like that. They might not need any instruction or training, but they will need plenty of support, encouragement, and friendship.

I once knew a young woman who was a member of the high school orchestra. A fine violinist, Vicki was also very timid. When she was asked to perform a solo at the school Christmas concert, she was almost too afraid even to try. She played so beautifully that she would have needed little extra practice to prepare, but she was frightened of playing before a large audience.

Vicki's teacher, though, was an inspired leader. He built her confidence by having her play in front of the violin section and then in front of the entire orchestra. These were people Vicki knew, and she wasn't quite as timid playing for them. Through lots of support and encouragement, both from her teacher and from her friends, Vicki played a beautiful solo at the concert.

People like Vicki need lots of encouragement. Be sure you give them the support and friendship they need to succeed.

You may also lead people who are not only willing to do the job but who are also very able. Let them get to it! Your best service to them will be to make sure they understand your expectations and then to provide plenty of opportunities for them to work.

When I was earning my pilot's license, I often practiced takeoffs and landings with my instructor. As we lifted off one time and were climbing out, the tone of the engine suddenly changed. Doing as I was taught, I pulled at the carburetor heat knob—and pulled it completely out of the instrument panel.

We were less than a thousand feet high, and I knew we had to land immediately. So, lowering the nose to maintain airspeed, I banked quickly to the left and made straight in for a short, crosswind runway where I landed safely.

My instructor sat calmly in his seat the entire time. He didn't do anything more than man the radio so I could be free to fly the plane. I *know* that he wanted to jump in and take over. It probably took every last ounce of willpower he had not to. But by letting me bring the plane in alone, he let me prove that I could handle myself in an emergency. That was a lesson I needed to have. He was ready to jump in and help at any time, but he knew that as long as I was flying correctly, he might as well sit back and let me.

An eighteen-year-old Eagle Scout named Jason used to spend his summers working at a Boy Scout camp. And he was good at it. Many of his friends also spent their summers there, and there was little about the camp that they didn't know very well.

One summer a new man came to direct the camp. Mr. Harston was a good camp director, but he was blunt and forceful. When he wanted something done, he'd explain in great detail everything he wanted and then he'd stand by and watch to make certain it was done exactly right.

But Jason and his friends were used to being trusted. They were good workers, and they resented being ordered around and watched over so carefully. A few of them began protesting, and morale in the camp dropped to an all-time low. Finally, Mr. Harston took Jason aside one day for a talk.

"Things aren't working out so well," Mr. Harston began.

Jason nodded. "I know."

"I'd like to hear what you think the reasons are."

Jason took a deep breath. "Well, I've been working here for a long time. So have most of the other guys. We all know our jobs and we think we do them pretty well. Before, we've always been allowed to do our work. But you watch over us like a hawk. You act like you don't trust us. You treat us like a bunch of little kids."

Mr. Harston smiled. "I've spent the last five years directing Camp Walker," he said. "It's a smaller camp than this one, and the boys who work there are a lot younger than you are. I've always had to keep close tabs on them to make certain everything was done right."

Jason and Mr. Harston were now looking at each other. For the first time, they were beginning to understand one another. Jason's friends were young men who were both willing and able to do their jobs. They needed the opportunity to be left alone to do them. Mr. Harston, on the other hand, was used to dealing with boys who were willing but not quite able, boys who needed extensive training, instruction, and supervision.

For the first time, Jason realized that his boss wasn't a mean old ogre. He was just a man who had never worked with a highly qualified staff before. And, for the first time, Mr. Harston realized that Jason's staff wasn't a bunch of troublemakers. They were just young men who knew what they were doing and who needed to be left alone to do it.

Morale in the camp suddenly changed. Jason convinced his friends to tolerate Mr. Harston's need to watch over them. Mr. Harston gave the young men more freedom to work. And when Mr. Harston saw that his staff could indeed do their work without supervision, he let them do it.

Before you start ordering people around, find out how

much they can do. Give them a few small tasks, if you
need to, to find out just what abilities they have. Then
adjust your leadership methods accordingly. If they know
what you want and they know how to do it, let 'em. If
they can do it but they lack confidence, encourage 'em. If
they want to do it but don't yet know how, train 'em. And
don't be afraid to let others help out, too. Giving group
members a chance to work and a chance to prove themselves will boost morale and confidence, and it will help
to make your group the very best it can be.

Things to Do Now!

• Take a good look at the people you lead. Decide what
  abilities they have. If they know what to do, learn to let
  them do it. If they need encouragement, learn to stand
  by them. If they need training, learn to teach them.

• Remember that nice coaches win as often as mean ones.
  But nice ones are usually liked better. Learn to be a nice
  coach. If you need to yell, yell encouragement.

12

GETTING RID OF TICKS
Effective Counseling

T he Colorado River is good for more than just riding rapids. It's great for washing dishes.

Filling my second bucket full of the cardboard-colored water and setting it on the stove to heat, I surveyed the knot of people standing around the dinner table about ten feet away. This was our fourth day on the river, and after a long day of shooting rapids, everyone was hungry.

I turned back to my wash water and was moving the bucket to a better spot on the stove when a fifteen-year-old boy named Bryan walked over.

"Got a minute?" he asked.

"Sure. Need something?"

Bryan scuffed his right shoe in the sand and shrugged. "I'd just like to talk to you for a minute if you're not busy."

I wiped my hands dry and nodded. Bryan was a boy usually full of life and energy, I reflected. This was the first time I remembered seeing him without a smile. I figured something must be wrong.

"Not busy at all," I said. "Let's go for a walk."

Bryan was unusually quiet as we walked away from camp and over a small ridge. And I worried about what might be troubling him. So when I thought we were a comfortable distance from camp, I asked, "How's everything going?"

Bryan shrugged. "Okay, I guess."

"Are you enjoying the trip?"

"Yeah. Pretty much." He paused. "But I've got a problem."

"Want to talk about it?"

He hesitated for a moment and his face turned red. "Promise you won't tell?"

I nodded. "Promise."

Bryan hesitated another moment.

"I've got a wood tick."

A wave of relief flooded over me. Bryan's solemn manner had convinced me that I was in for a heavy-duty counseling session. And I hated the thought of his struggling with some inner turmoil: he was too nice a kid to be bothered with serious problems. But a wood tick! I tried not to grin.

Because I live in tick-thick country, I'd seen dozens of wood ticks. And I knew that when you're careful, they're usually not much trouble to get rid of.

But to Bryan, having a wood tick was the worst thing in the world. He was certain the little pest would have to be cut out by a doctor, and he was scared to death of needles, scalpels, and other medical equipment. When I told him I could oust the tiny beast just by dabbing on a little ointment, he breathed a sigh as if all the burdens in the world had just been lifted from his shoulders.

I was lucky. When Bryan first came to talk with me, we were both certain that the end of the world was close at hand. What a great feeling it was to find a quick solution to the problem and have it over with. Even though it was all over in just a few minutes, it drew Bryan and me closer together as friends.

As a leader, you too will have many opportunities to deal with the problems of others. Each individual has his or her own set of problems. And when these individuals join your group, they'll bring those problems with them. Be ready with an ear to listen and a shoulder to lean on if they need it.

A young neighbor of mine once came to ask some advice about school. Denise was a bubbly thirteen-year-old in the eighth grade. She was a member of the student council, and she could talk the ears off Mr. Spock. As she told me about life in junior high, she laughed and joked about her history teacher, telling me that she was doing poorly in his class, and I was surprised when I suddenly noticed tears. I knew that people sometimes shed tears of happiness. But even though Denise was laughing, I had a hunch her tears were not happy ones.

"You're worried about it, aren't you?"

Denise wiped at her tears and tried to keep up the smile, but couldn't.

"I'm getting As and Bs in all my other classes," she said. "But Mr. Wright is giving me a D!"

Denise went on to tell me that she tried hard in history, but no matter how much work she did she couldn't seem to make things work out. She'd been on the honor roll every term since seventh grade, and she'd never had a grade lower than a B–. To suddenly be faced with a D was more than she wanted to think about.

And her parents—she didn't dare tell them yet, she said. She knew they wouldn't be mad at her, but she didn't want to disappoint them. Her parents valued high grades, and they had always been proud of her efforts.

And the student council! If she received a D, her grade average might be too low to stay on the student council!

I knew how Denise was feeling. As insignificant as a D might seem, there are some situations where one can nearly be fatal. I nearly received a D in a college physics class. It was during my last semester of school, and it was a required class. Any grade lower than a C– wouldn't have counted, and I wouldn't have graduated. My entire college career boiled down to a mere couple of points in physics!

I didn't tell Denise any of this. I just listened as she continued to talk. I knew how I felt when I faced my D, and I remembered how much I longed for someone to share my problems with.

After several minutes, Denise mentioned that her history teacher was the only person who could really help her. She asked if I thought she should talk it over with him.

I nodded. And with that, Denise smiled and left. A few days later she was back with a plate of chocolate chip cookies.

"Thanks for helping me," she said. "I went and talked with Mr. Wright and guess what?"

"What?"

"I wasn't even getting a D in the first place! It was a mistake!"

"Well, good for you!"

"Anyway, I wanted to say thanks again for helping me."

I didn't say anything, but I really hadn't done much helping. All I'd done was listen. I had given her a chance to talk about her worries, and I had shown her that I cared.

That's all that most people need. After all, they understand their problems a lot better than anyone else. And being able to talk about them is sometimes all they need to feel better. Sometimes that's all they need to find a solution.

Sharie, a high school sophomore taking an algebra class, once asked an older friend named Marilyn to help her with a difficult problem. As Marilyn watched, Sharie wrote the problem and explained what she needed to do. As she described each step, her eyes suddenly lit up.

"Oh, my gosh!" she said. "I see what I've been doing wrong!"

And with that she went to finish her homework without any problem. Marilyn didn't do a single thing to help, but she got all the credit for the answer! Besides that, Marilyn boosted Sharie's confidence by letting her solve the problem herself.

It's hard not to give advice when someone has problems, but it's important that you don't. As much as it hurts to see someone struggling for answers, you won't be helping by making decisions for him or her. And unless you know all the facts—a rare possibility!—you could even make things worse by making the wrong decision.

Instead, just listen. Let the person vent concerns, worries, and frustrations. Acknowledge those feelings. Show the person that you care.

It's important, too, that you don't take sides when someone comes to you with a problem. If the person is upset or angry, he or she is probably not going to give you an accurate picture of the situation. And by jumping to conclusions you could do someone else great harm.

A better idea is to remain neutral.

If someone tells you that "Mrs. Galbraith called me a nerd! Right in front of the whole class!" don't say, "Boy, she really is a jerk, isn't she?"

Instead, say something like, "Boy, you must have been mad!"

By doing this you keep the conversation neutral. You recognize your friend's feelings without taking sides. You'll help to calm him rather than to fuel his anger.

Many times people just need the chance to spout a little steam. They need the opportunity to vent their concerns, worries, and angers. By listening to them you can help to relieve their frustrations. By not fueling their emotions you can help to calm their feelings and learn to cope with the situation.

There will be many times when people will act quite differently. They might want someone to talk with but might not dare to ask. Maybe they don't want to bother you, or maybe they're just frightened. But if you're tuned in to those you lead, you'll know when they have a problem. They might appear sad or moody. They may not act as happy as they usually are.

If you suspect that members of your group have something on their mind, let them know that you're willing to listen. But don't force them to talk. If they're not ready to share their feelings, it's best that you don't try to make them. Instead, show them increased friendship and understanding. Show them you care. And when they're ready to talk, they'll come to you.

There was a time while I was in college when everything seemed to be going wrong for me. I was working hard in my classes and at my job, but even so, rewards were few and far between. I became sad and moody.

One day a good friend of mine named Paul came to visit me in my office. He locked the door behind him, took my phone off the hook, and looked me square in the eyes.

"What's wrong?" he asked.

"What do you mean?"

"I mean you. There's something wrong. I haven't seen you laugh or smile in a week. I know you. I can tell when there's something wrong."

Paul's approach was blunt—maybe too blunt for most people—but it was just what I needed at the time. Sitting back in his chair, he showed that he was ready to listen. And he sat there for nearly an hour as I poured out my soul to him.

There's a great blessing that comes from counseling—and from being counseled. Baring your soul to someone draws the two of you closer together. Think about a time that you've talked your problems out with someone who really listened. Afterward, didn't you feel closer to that person than when you started? I certainly did!

Counseling is a healthy process that's good for both people. When you learn to counsel effectively—when you show through your undivided interest that you really do care—the two of you will grow closer. You'll build a bond of friendship, gratitude, and mutual respect that will last a lifetime.

Things to Do Now!

• Learn to be a listener. Practice listening. When people know that you're a good listener, they'll be more confident coming to you with problems.

• Watch your group members for mood swings that might indicate a need for counseling. Even if there isn't a problem, they'll see that you really are concerned about them.

• Remember to remain neutral. Listen when people are angry, but don't fuel the fire!

13

CAMPING IN THE RAIN

The Need for
Evaluating

Tom Baugh shrugged off his heavy backpack and looked for a place to set it. Heavy rain lashed at the forest all around him, and sharp forks of lightning bit through the night sky.

Tom paused as a crack of thunder boomed over the mountain, and then he took his two-man tent and began setting it up. He didn't have anyone camping with him that night, but he wasn't on a normal camping trip, either. Tom was, in fact, evaluating backpacking gear. He had gone out into the mountain thunderstorm because he had a certain tent that he needed to try out.

"A lot of backpackers have to set up camp after dark and in storms," Tom told me. "And I needed to see how this tent would cooperate."

Tom said he was worried that by pitching the tent in the middle of a storm, he would get everything wet. But he was surprised. Even though it was dark and he had no one to help him, the tent went up so fast the storm didn't have a chance.

"It was an easy tent to pitch," Tom said. "I'd pitched it before in daylight so I had a good idea of what I was doing. The tent is designed so simply that there wasn't any guesswork. I just laid it out, slipped the poles into the sleeves, and bingo! It was up."

After tightening down the rain fly, Tom took his backpack and stuffed it inside. He spent a few minutes getting ready for bed, then took a flashlight and checked every seam he could find for leaks. There weren't any.

Over the next couple of months Tom spent a lot of time with that tent, and with many others. He filled notebooks with his impressions of them. He knew which ones were good and which ones weren't. Most important, he knew *why* they were good or not.

That was all part of a research project. By reading Tom's evaluations, manufacturers learned how well their gear worked. They learned which features worked well and which needed improvement.

We improve our leadership in much the same way. By evaluating our progress, we learn what things we do well and what things we need to do better.

After you finish a job, analyze what happened. If things went well, find out why. Then the next time you have an assignment, you'll have a good idea of what things to try again.

But if things didn't go so well, decide why not. And the next time you have a job, you'll know what sort of things to avoid. Only when you evaluate your performance can you expect to improve.

I used to work with a young woman who was on the high school debate team. After every tournament Julie sat down with her teammates and carefully evaluated the meet. They talked about what things worked well and what didn't. They talked about tactics that were effective and plans that bombed. They learned by experience how to present certain ideas, and they learned tricks their opponents were likely to spring on them. By the time they reached the state tournament, they were as polished as a team could get.

Evaluation is one of the most important keys to leadership because it is the step in which we learn. We try something, and if it works, we find ways to make it better. If it doesn't work, we haven't failed—we have simply learned what *doesn't* work.

A friend who spent many years as a sportswriter said he used to bristle at the idea of someone editing his stories. But he soon learned that good writers appreciate good editors.

"I found out that no matter how well I wrote a story," he said, "a good editor could always make it better. And I liked that."

Instead of being offended when an editor changed his copy, Steve found out why the editor changed it. By carefully reading his stories after they had been edited, and by learning why certain changes had been made, he became a better writer. As time went on, his editors made fewer and fewer corrections. And soon he was allowed to send his work out without having it edited at all.

Be aggressive in evaluating yourself. Learn what things you do well, and repeat them. Learn what things you need help with, and improve them.

Being evaluated is often hard. Most of us live for praise and encouragement, and listening to someone outline our faults isn't much fun. But we all have to take our lumps sometime, so don't be afraid of it! Instead, when something goes wrong, make the most of it. Analyze why it went wrong, and ask yourself, "What can I learn from this? What can I do better next time?"

I once knew a diver who was, well, awful. Greg belonged to a club that didn't have a good coaching staff, and no one ever took the time to tell him just how bad he was. He did manage to win a few ribbons at local meets, and that led him to think of himself as average — which was stretching things quite a bit. When he won, it was because no one else showed up who was any good.

One time, though, while Greg was warming up for a meet, a diver from another club came up and began talking with him.

"You know," he said, "if you'd kiss the board instead of jumping clear into the middle of the pool, you'd have more time to execute your dives."

Greg was surprised. "What do you mean?"

"Well, to do a dive really well, you've got to get as much height off the board as you can. But when you dive, you jump *out* instead of *up*."

"Really?"

The diver nodded. "Yeah. And you know what else would help?"

Greg shook his head. "No. What?"

"When you make your hurdle, try to keep your body straight and rigid. That way you won't absorb as much spring from the board, and it'll give you a better jump."

Because it was the first time anyone had really evaluated his dives, Greg listened closely. Not only that, but he took the suggestions to heart. He worked to improve his hurdle, and he concentrated on jumping up rather than out. He also began asking other divers to watch him, and by acting on their observations he became a better diver.

As you progress in your leadership, you'll find many opportunities to evaluate those you lead, too. Some leaders are good at this, and some aren't. Some evaluate too harshly, looking only for things that go wrong. Others are too kind, noticing only what goes well. But neither leader is doing much good. If you focus on others' mistakes, they may feel picked on. If you mention only their good points, they may never improve.

A good evaluation must cover both good points and bad. Make sure you praise your group for things they've done well. And make sure they know what things they can do better.

If you feel uncomfortable about this kind of evaluation (as many of us do!), then let the group evaluate itself. You'll find that in many cases the group members already know what went right. And they usually know where they goofed up, too. So instead of telling them what they already know, simply direct the conversation with a few questions.

"Well, what went best for you today?"

"Anything go wrong?"

"What could you have done differently?"

"What things should you try again next time?"

To get everyone really thinking, don't forget to throw in the question "Why?" Everyone may realize that a certain activity was the hit of the party, but only when they stop to figure out *why* it was popular will they be able to find other, similar activities. And only by deciding why something went sour will they be able to avoid other, similar mistakes in the future.

When Penn State played Miami for the national football championship at the end of the 1986 season, Penn State was picked to lose the game by a touchdown. After all, Miami hadn't lost a game all season, and the Hurricanes featured some of the top players in the country.

But the Penn State coaches knew that every team had its weaknesses. In the final weeks before the game, they spent long hours watching films of the Hurricanes, evaluating how they played and how they reacted to certain situations. They noticed, for instance, that when Miami's receivers were jammed at the line, they lost their confidence. And they noticed that in dire situations, Miami's quarterback stared at the receiver he was going to throw to.

So late in the game, when the Hurricanes had the ball

fourth-and-goal on the 13, Penn State watched the quarterback's eyes. The score was 14-10 for Penn State. If Miami made this play, the Hurricanes would win. The national championship boiled down to one play.

By the way Miami lined up, Penn State knew the Hurricanes were going to pass. And they knew the quarterback would give away his target. At the snap Penn State dropped eight men to the goal line, and they watched the quarterback. He had three receivers running for the end zone, but he looked at only one of them. The Lions converged on that player and intercepted the ball before it reached him. They won the championship.

Penn State had a team full of great players. But it was by evaluating their opponents that they *knew* how to beat them. And the upset was ranked as one of the greatest games of the season.

As a leader, you'll have many successes. And you will probably make a few mistakes, too; all of us do. But as you begin to evaluate your performance and learn from your experiences, you'll find more successes and fewer mistakes.

As you evaluate your progress, remember to find the reasons for your successes as well as the reasons for your failures. When you've done something right, you'll want to do it again!

Things to Do Now!

- Decide not to worry about mistakes you make. Instead, treat them as learning opportunities. Learn what you can from each of them, and resolve to do better next time!

- Evaluate your progress as a leader. List both your strong points and weak points.

- After your next group project, carefully evaluate what happened. Make a list of which things went right and which went wrong. Determine why certain ideas worked or failed, and use this information when planning your next project.

- Ask your group to evaluate itself. Remember to ask for strengths *and* weaknesses. And don't forget the question "Why?"

14

SAYING THANK YOU

Giving Positive Feedback

Mrs. Shaha walked up to the boy sitting in the third row and tapped him on the shoulder. "Rob, would you mind staying for a few minutes after class?"

Rob shook his head. "No. Not at all."

Rob's friends snickered as Mrs. Shaha walked back to her desk. And Rob worried about what his English teacher wanted. He was sure he was up on his assignments. He knew his latest compositions had been well written. And he had been scoring well on tests and quizzes. He couldn't imagine what was wrong.

The class period passed slowly, but finally the bell rang and Rob's friends filed from the room. Rob waited until everyone had left and then approached his teacher. "You wanted to talk to me?"

Mrs. Shaha nodded. "Yes, Rob. I wanted to tell you that I called your father this morning."

Rob felt his heart sink. That was all he needed.

"I wanted to tell him about your work," Mrs. Shaha continued. "Because I've never had a student who writes as well as you do."

Rob looked up sharply. "What?"

"You're a tremendous young man, Rob," the teacher said. "And you have a gift for writing. I told your father it would be a shame to see such talent wasted. I said he should encourage you to find every opportunity to polish your skills."

Rob left the room with an ear-to-ear smile. His teacher had gone out of her way to do what she did, and it made Rob feel terrific. He loved writing. And he had secret hopes of someday writing for magazines. To have his teacher praise him as she had gave him a surge of confidence.

There is no motivation quite so powerful as positive reinforcement. You don't think so? Take a minute and go looking through one of your drawers. Find any merit badges? Ribbons? Certificates? Newspaper clippings with your name on them?

Think of the work it took to earn those items. I still have the certificate I won in a high school math contest. I spent hours and hours preparing for that contest. And all I got for it was a simple certificate. But the satisfaction of winning that certificate was worth millions.

People enjoy recognition, even when they receive nothing more than a blue ribbon or a piece of paper with their name on it. People enjoy being noticed. Think how good it makes you feel when someone notices or mentions something you've done. You can make someone else feel that same way. It isn't what you say or reward them with that matters. It's just the fact that you noticed.

I used to work with a young woman who always wore a certain ring. It wasn't an expensive ring—it wasn't even her best ring—but it was the one she wore. It was her favorite. Why? It was given to her by our employer as a reward for hard work.

When you find times to praise the members of your

group, remember it's not how much you give them. It's just the fact that you recognize them. A small token of thanks is just as effective as something very expensive.

The power of positive feedback can also prevent many discipline problems. When a person knows there's a chance for praise, he's likely to do his very best work. Even people who are known for being lazy or causing trouble are likely to work if they have a chance to be praised.

Remember that you're not just trying to motivate your top workers. Many of them will be doing their very best anyway. What you want is to nudge those along who might lack motivation or desire.

There are a few guidelines.

First, give your praise immediately. Don't wait until the end of the week to recognize a good deed. Do it now!

A junior high school science teacher made it a habit to walk around the room as his students worked. He'd look at what everyone was doing and make comments as he went.

"Nice work, there, Mary . . . You've got that just right, Steve . . . Very neat material, Lisa."

He didn't just disappear behind his desk as many teachers do, but he got right out in the room and offered feedback. He let his students know right then that they were doing good things.

Second, remember to praise small triumphs as well as big ones. After all, small ones lead to big ones. And they are just as important.

My friend Linda had been practicing a dance routine for several weeks. Part of her dance included a triple turn that she had a lot of trouble with. She couldn't do it without falling.

Her teacher kept encouraging her, and Linda kept working on it. One day she was practicing her routine when—voilà!—she did the triple turn!

As soon as she finished the dance, her teacher gave her a hug and handed her a pair of movie tickets. "Congratulations!" she said.

The triple turn was only a very small part of a complex dance number. But Linda's teacher knew how important it was to Linda. By recognizing her — even with something as simple as a hug and movie tickets — she made it clear that she was as thrilled with Linda's success as Linda was.

Third, be unpredictable. Surprise can make many rewards far more effective. When a school class learns that by giving the teacher an apple they are going to be given a break, their effort isn't sincere. They'll be bringing apples just to be bringing apples.

And your praise shouldn't be considered payment for a job well done. Instead, it should be seen as a way of saying: "Hey! You're okay! And I appreciate what you're doing!"

Finally, be specific. Don't just say, "This is for a good job, Steve." Instead, say: "Your poster was the most creative one I've ever seen." Or, "This is for baking the best chocolate chip cookies I've ever eaten."

When the rewards are many, and people believe the possibility of earning them is high, the average person will stretch to achieve them. It doesn't matter if the rewards are big or small. When people get praised for doing something right, they'll be out beating the bushes to do it again.

I remember in high school having a math teacher who asked us to begin work on a page with about forty problems.

"I'll give you twenty minutes to work on them," he said. Many of us — most of us, actually — moaned. But the teacher just smiled and said, "And I'll give you double points for every correct problem you do past number fifteen."

The moaning stopped immediately as we all bent into our work. We received bonus points only for the last half of the assignment — and we had to finish the first half first — so we were all racing to get there. Because our teacher graded mostly on tests and quizzes, the bonus points we were earning didn't really amount to much, but that didn't stop us from working. We had a chance for a reward, and we were going for it. Each of us had an equal chance to succeed, and each of us could decide exactly how far to go.

On a week-long backpacking trek, a guide named Rick developed a morale-boosting method of offering feedback. He knew that because everyone was sharing tents, there would be some questions about who had to pack the tent every day. After all, they were hiking through rugged country, and even a five-pound tent makes a lot of difference when you're climbing up the side of a rocky mountain.

The first morning out, Rick had everyone line up. Then he said, "Okay. I'd like everyone who is packing a tent this morning to step forward."

Seven boys looked up and stepped forward.

"For being good sports and volunteering to pack tents on our first day on the trail, I'd like to present each of you with the coveted Heavy Pack award." With that he handed each of the boys a bagful of raisins to eat on the trail.

The raisins weren't reward enough to make anyone *want* to lug a heavy tent around. But they proved to everyone that Rick noticed and appreciated the effort.

The next evening, as everyone was sitting around the campfire telling stories, Rick asked, "Who made dinner tonight?" When two boys raised their hands, Rick said: "That was the best trail dinner I've eaten in a long time. For cooking above and beyond the call of hunger, I'd like to give each of you a bag of raisins."

A few days later, during a dry camp, four boys hiked a mile or so to a fresh water source to fill a couple of water bottles for breakfast the next morning. When they returned, Rick was ready with more raisins.

Rick was effective for several reasons. He gave his awards right away. He rewarded small deeds as well as big ones. He was unpredictable: he didn't give awards for the same things every day. Instead he tried to make the awards spontaneous and meaningful. He let everyone know that he was looking for good behavior and that he was noticing their efforts.

Rick was much of the reason that everyone had a good time on the trail.

At girls' camp a counselor did much the same thing. Every day — while the campers were busy with activities — Marci inspected the cabins. If a girl's bed was made and everything left neatly, Marci left a white feather on the pillow with a thank-you note. If she saw someone doing a favor for someone else, she secretly slipped a note and a prize into the girl's pocket.

She never told anyone what she was doing, and she never signed her notes, so no one ever knew who was doing this. But when a girl went out of her way to help someone else on the trail, she'd return to find a white feather on her pillow with a note with a simple message like, "Thanks so much for helping Bonnie today."

A little word of thanks or recognition is often all it takes to boost someone's spirits. It gives people a chance to grow a little, to feel success, and to feel good about themselves. And when you treat people like A+ people, they'll give you A+ work — or at least *their* very best effort — in return.

Things to Do Now!

- Remember that every person in your group has the ability to do something well. Find that something and praise him for it.

- Say something positive to each person you lead. Look for their triumphs and successes. Don't let a day go by without complimenting each one on something.

- Be sincere. Learn to appreciate each person's successes.

- Find a simple reward system to show your appreciation for good effort. It doesn't have to be elaborate. Something as simple as notes or white feathers is as effective as expensive prizes.

- Give your best appreciation to those you lead. See if their best doesn't come back to you!

15

A LESSON IN HUGS

The Importance
of Love

D̲ax Anderson came run-
ning up the driveway and into the garage.

"Are you leaving? Today?"

I tossed a sleeping bag into the back of my truck and
nodded. "Yeah. I've got to pick up my partner in an hour."

Dax, ten years old at the time and wearing his favorite
tennis outfit, looked disappointed.

"How long will you be gone?"

"Ten days." I thought for a moment. "I'll be back a
week from Wednesday."

"So long?" Dax frowned.

I nodded. And I frowned, too. Dax lived a couple of
houses down the street from me. We often played tennis
together after school, and we spent a lot of time sitting
around the backyard telling stories. During the ten days I
was gone, I would miss him.

Dax helped me finish loading my truck. "Well," I said.
"I think that'll do it. Thanks for your help."

"Sure."

Just then, Dax's mother called. He turned. "Well, I've got to go. I'll see you next week."

"Okay. 'Bye, Dax."

"'Bye."

He turned and began running for home. He had gone only a little way before he stopped and came running back. He jumped up and threw his arms around me.

"Be careful," he said. "I'll be praying for you."

The next ten days were hard ones for me. I was leading a section of the national camping school, and I faced problem after problem. Heavy rains forced me to change schedules nearly every day. One of my students developed serious medical problems on the trail. Supplies I depended on never arrived.

But throughout everything, one thought kept cropping up. I kept hearing Dax say, "I'll be praying for you."

It's amazing what the power of love can do for a person. And knowing that back home a ten-year-old boy was praying for me kept me going, even when everything else seemed to be going wrong. Dax's simple love fueled me for ten grueling days.

Dax wasn't a leader of mine, but he influenced me in many ways. And his love for me motivated me, inspired me, and made me want to be at my best at all times. I would have done anything for him.

Think how you feel when someone does something special for you. Think of the warmth you feel when you know that somebody really loves you.

You can make someone else feel that same way.

To be an effective leader, you must love those you lead. You must show them that you love them. You'll find that nothing will motivate them quite so well.

I have a couple of friends named John and Matt. John has two of the most obnoxious little brothers anyone could ever have, and Matt hated visiting John's home—just because he knew John's brothers would be there.

One day, though, while John was away at college, Matt told me that he was taking John's brothers fishing. I couldn't believe it.

"But you hate them!"

"Not really," he said. "I used to, but I found out that they're really not all that bad."

I still couldn't believe it.

"What changed your mind?"

Matt pushed his hands in his pockets and shook his head. "I found out they liked me."

It's hard to hate someone who likes you. It's hard not to like someone who loves you. The simple fact that John's little brothers liked him completely changed Matt's attitude.

People's attitudes change when they know you like them. People like being loved! And—with enough time—even the most hardened person will return those feelings.

Aaron Cross told me a story about his college geology teacher that proves a similar point.

During his first year at the university, Aaron signed up for a difficult geology course. Like many other college classes, it was taught in an auditorium. And there were more than one hundred students in the class.

The first thing the professor did was make a seating chart. He let everyone choose a seat, and then he wrote everyone's name down. Within a couple of weeks he was calling everyone by name—without the use of his chart. When he returned tests and papers, he passed them out individually—all one hundred of them—without the use of his chart. Memorizing everyone's names must have been an awful chore. But by doing so the professor showed his students that he really cared.

"It was funny," Aaron told me. "Just the fact that he was walking up to me, calling me by name and handing me my papers made me want to do better on them. I knew I wasn't just a face in the crowd to him. I would have been embarrassed if I had a low score."

What a lesson in motivation! If Aaron's teacher could motivate students just by knowing their names, think what you could do with a lot of loving and caring!

At a high school tennis camp, two young women became close friends. Toward the end of camp, while Kristine was taking some pointers in serving, Tracy became sick. Leaving the courts she went back to her room and curled up in bed with a very upset stomach. She hadn't been there long before Kristine suddenly burst into the room

"I heard you were sick," she said. "So I came as fast as I could."

There wasn't much that Kristine could do to help. But the fact that she cared enough to come was all that Tracy needed.

"I would do anything for Kristine," Tracy told me, "because I know that she really cares about me. I love her as much as anyone I know."

I once took my friend Duke down to the airport to look at the planes. We spent more than an hour crawling through cockpits, looking under wings, and watching take-offs.

As we walked out onto the tarmac, Duke, who is nine, took my hand. He held onto it as we visited hangars and looked around.

After a while he looked up and asked, "Do you mind if I hold your hand?"

No, indeed! By holding my hand he was sending me a message. He was saying, "I like you!"

What a powerful message! What a great feeling it is to *know* that you're loved! And like Tracy, I wanted to return the love I received.

Feeling the love of another person creates such strong feelings of friendship and goodwill that it's hard not to return them. It's hard not to share them. It's hard not to burst with love for everyone around us.

Of course, we can't go around holding people's hands

and giving them hugs as much as we'd like—or even as much as we should. But there are different ways of doing the same thing. You can do it with notes, if you want to. It takes only a minute and it has the same marvelous effect.

A simple message such as "Great game!" or "Good Luck!" is just the ticket. No matter what you write, the message is still the same: "I like you!"

It's a message that no one ever tires of hearing.

And if you really want to make it fun, be clever. Instead of just walking up and handing someone a note, hide it in a shoe or hang it in a locker. It doesn't have to be long. Just a line or two will do it.

When I was serving my mission, I received a small Christmas package from my parents. Inside were dozens of tiny matchboxes, each wrapped like tiny Christmas gifts. They made no noise when I shook them and I wondered what could be in them. It bugged me for days. And on Christmas morning they were the first things I turned to.

Inside each box was a note from one of my friends at home. There was one from my dentist, one from a school teacher, one from the family vet. Some were from girls I had dated. Others were from people I had worked with. All of them were from people I missed.

None of the notes was more than a couple of lines long. But they were my most welcomed Christmas gifts. Just knowing that so many people were pulling for me, thinking of me, and praying for my success was enough to charge my batteries for many weeks.

When I was in college, I worked as a sportswriter. I worked for the university's Sports Information Office, and I wrote for a couple of local newspapers at the same time.

Going to school and working so many hours was hard. And I remember one time becoming especially discouraged. For several days in a row I had left for school before 8:00 A.M. and hadn't returned home until after 8:00 P.M. That didn't leave much time for doing anything else.

Besides that, nothing seemed to be going very right for me. My classes were hard, and I didn't seem to be doing all that well in them. I was given tight deadlines for almost everything I wrote at work, so I didn't have time to make my stories as good as I usually did.

After several days of this, I returned home from a ball game one night feeling discouraged. Nothing seemed to be fun anymore. Nothing I did seemed to be worth the effort. No one seemed to appreciate anything that I did. That was all a heavy burden for me. And I was feeling pretty low.

But a couple of weeks before I had taken a young friend of mine named Bryan on an overnight campout. He had been going through some rough times himself, and he had asked to spend a little time alone with me. We had hiked to a remote spot that we both liked and spent the evening talking and watching stars.

I hadn't seen him since.

But as I walked up to my home, tired, discouraged, and wishing that I could just go to bed and put a merciful end to the day, I found a note taped to the door. The message was simple and direct.

Dear Shane,
Thanks for being my friend. You're just like a big brother to me.
Love,
Bryan

Those two simple sentences did more for me than anything else could have. It was just the medicine I needed. And late as it was, I spent several hours that night polishing up stories and feeling good about myself.

I later realized that I could work that same magic on other people. And so can you. If you like someone, tell him. If you appreciate something that someone has done, tell her. Your love will go far in brightening other people's lives. It will set you apart as a true leader.

Take a minute and write the note. Say the word. Make the call. You can brighten someone's day. You can change someone's life.

And it only takes a second.

Things to Do Now!

- Write a note to someone you love. Let that person know that you're a friend.

- Think of something positive about every person in the group you lead. The next time you're alone with each of them, tell them!

- Don't be afraid to show your feelings. If someone's done a good job, tell him. If you like or appreciate someone, tell her. Now!

16

BEING A BATTERY CHARGER
Generating Enthusiasm

Stacey McDaniels took the inbounds pass and in a burst of energy bolted down the court. Her teammates wheeled through the lane as she crossed the midcourt line and called out a play for the low post.

"No mistakes now! Screen! Screen! C'mon, Leslie, post up! Move! Move!"

Running up and down the court while directing an explosive offense at the same time, Stacey was tiring to watch. But she wasn't about to slow down. With twin ponytails flailing the air behind her, she whipped a pass down the baseline, cut into the lane to set up the pick, shuffled left, raced right, then darted back to the left again, shouting to her teammates the whole time.

"Lisa! Watch the key! Move the ball, now, move the ball . . ."

A point guard on an all-girl team, Stacey had already

scored a game high of seventeen points, captured four rebounds, and forced three turnovers. Even when she was on the sidelines, she was a running flurry of action, pacing up and down the gym, clapping her hands, and keeping up that nonstop stream of talk.

"Good play, Pilots! Good play! Take the post, now, Nicole, take the post! Screen! Screen!"

And now, with her team leading by seven points, Stacey was still guiding the Pilots' offense. Taking a pass from underneath she cut back to the outside, faked with her head and shoulders, then sent the ball winging into the basket.

Whether her team was winning or not, Stacey always played like a can of pop: full of fizz and ready to burst with energy. She sparked such intensity among her teammates that the entire team played with furious enthusiasm.

You probably know people like Stacey. People who are always smiling. People who have the energy and enthusiasm to fire up their friends. People who don't complain when the weather is bad or when things go against them but who do whatever it takes to make the situation better. People who are fun to be around.

I like to call these people Number Ones. They bring out the best in their friends and teammates. They help others to be Number Ones. Like human whirlwinds, they sweep into their work and fire their friends up with energy and enthusiasm. As a leader, you'd be wise to keep a couple of Number Ones around you. Better yet, be one yourself, and those you lead may follow your example.

You probably know a few Number Twos as well. They're the people you hear moaning and groaning whenever things aren't going exactly right. They skip assignments, and they don't smile much.

Number Threes, unfortunately, are just as plentiful as Number Twos. But more than just complaining when there's a job to do, they are often openly antagonistic.

Many times they'll refuse to work at all, and they'll try to get others to quit, too. Sadly enough, many Number Three types become leaders, and they can often take a good experience and make it miserable.

The difference between these three types of people is simply one of attitude. Decide now that you will be a Number One.

I used to spend my summers working as a guide on the Colorado River. And let me tell you that there's nothing that can fire up enthusiasm like crashing a boat into a boiling stretch of rapids.

But one week was very different. For five straight days rainstorms lashed the river. Passengers who came loaded with suntan lotion spent most of their time huddled beneath ponchos or sleeping in plastic tube tents. The trip would have been pretty miserable except for a boy named Tim.

Tim was thirteen years old. He had smooth, gunstock hair and a mouthful of braces that he flashed around like his most prized possessions. He was vigorous and exciting—a teenage speed blur, his mother said—and on our first day out he knew the names of everyone on board before we were even ten minutes down the river.

Because the Colorado River inside the Grand Canyon is exceptionally cold, our passengers relied on the hot Arizona sun to keep warm. But on this trip, black-bellied clouds blocked out the sun most of the time. So when we smashed our boat through the rapids and sent freezing water crashing all around, things got miserable in a hurry.

None of this bothered Tim. The first thing every morning he took up position at the front of the boat where things got the wettest. Flashing his braces he'd wait eagerly for us to get underway. And when we went slicing through the rapids, he'd shout and wave his arms like a bronc-busting cowboy at a rodeo.

One time, as the boat boomed down from a high wave,

another wall of ice-cold water shot up to meet us. The bow bit savagely into the wave, and for a moment Tim seemed to disappear. Almost instantly the boat was being slammed again into the waves as gallons of liquid ice crashed down upon us.

Through all of it, I kept seeing Tim's flashing smile as he shook the water from his gunstock hair and shouted, "More! More! Give us more!"

By the time we passed the rapids and were into smooth water again, I was laughing so hard at Tim that I could barely steer. It didn't matter that the sun wasn't shining. It didn't matter that the water was cold: I could hardly feel it. I was having fun! And so was everyone else. And the reason was Tim. His youthful enthusiasm was so contagious that everyone caught it. He kept the entire group perked up the entire time we were on the river.

I remember returning from a cross-country ski trip one January morning and trying to start my new Bronco. Because the temperature on the mountain was below freezing—and because it had been several days since it had last been fired up—the engine wouldn't start. It couldn't: the battery was dead. I had to borrow a pair of jumper cables and a friend's car battery to get my own started again.

People sometimes need their own batteries charged just like that. Work gets hard, and maybe they haven't had a pat on the back in quite a while. At these times, a person with an encouraging smile or a contagious sense of humor can lift them out of the doldrums.

You can be that person.

When you are a Number One type person—when you become a battery charger—your friends and those you lead will notice. They'll come to you for the simple reason that people like being with Number One types. People like battery chargers.

More to the point, when you are a Number One person you'll find that leadership becomes easy. When you make a suggestion, your friends will respond because your enthusiasm will make them enthusiastic. They will draw upon your energy. You'll be surprised at how many problems will just seem to disappear.

Enthusiasm is contagious.

A Boy Scout troop I work with once volunteered to haul several hundred pioneering poles up to a local Scout camp as a service project. Loading the poles into the back of the truck was a dirty, tiring job, and everyone was soon sapped of energy. By the time we reached the camp and were ready to unload, several boys were beginning to moan and grumble. It looked as if we were in for several hours of backbreaking work when a boy named Jeff climbed to the top of the load like the King of the Hill.

"You guys are all wimps!" he declared. "I bet I can throw poles out faster than any of you!"

His challenge was immediately accepted. Everyone else climbed to the ground, and Brad set the stopwatch on his digital wristwatch.

As Brad readied himself as timer, Jeff went through the motions of warming up, stretching his arms and flexing his fingers.

"I'll give you sixty seconds," Brad said in his most authoritative voice. "On your mark. Get set. GO!"

Jeff began heaving poles out of the truck as fast as he could. A minute later Brad yelled, "STOP!"

Jeff tossed one more log over the side, which the boys decided was an illegal pole. They picked it up and put it back in the truck.

"You got only seventeen poles," Darren said. "I can do better than that."

Darren managed only fourteen poles, and he wanted to try again, but the boys refused to allow him another turn until everyone had had a chance.

By the time everyone had taken a turn, Jeff's record of seventeen poles still stood, and by the time the truck had been emptied the boys were as full as excitement and energy as little kids at Christmas. With just a bit of creativity and a whole lot of enthusiasm, Jeff had taken a tedious chore and turned it into a fun-filled adventure. He had taken hard work and made a game of it.

When I was in eighth grade, I signed up for first-year algebra. Until then math had never been one of my strong subjects. It had never been one of my favorite subjects. And I wasn't looking forward to taking the class.

But there was a bright side. Many of my friends had also signed up for algebra, and several of us were assigned to the same class at the same time. One of these was a boy named Rhett.

Now, Rhett was one of those students who never had trouble in school. Our math teacher, Mr. Baugh, liked to call him an "Albert Einstein think-alike."

Part of Rhett's success was his enthusiasm. Instead of moaning when Mr. Baugh gave us an assignment, Rhett jumped right into it. Sometimes he'd lean over and say, "I'll bet I can finish faster than you can."

I knew he could finish faster than I could, but I'd race him anyway. It became a game, and I found myself listening more intently to Mr. Baugh's lectures so I'd be able to do the assigned problems as easily as possible. Racing against Rhett, I needed every bit of help I could get!

Algebra soon became my favorite class, and like Rhett, I was soon spreading enthusiasm for the subject. I'm not saying it was always easy, but through the excitement of a Number One type person, our entire class began seeing the fun in math, rather than the work.

Even battery chargers need to be charged themselves now and then. And it helps to find a special friend who has the ability to fire you up when you need it. My own battery charger is a ten-year-old boy named Jimmy. Spending a few minutes with Jimmy is like spending a few minutes with a firecracker. Whenever I need a charge—and even when I don't! — just by talking with Jimmy for a while I feel recharged and ready to go climb a mountain or something.

As you develop your own style of leadership, you'll find many chances to build enthusiasm yourself. The day may be cold and the job may be hard. And most likely there'll be lots of grumbling about it. But at times like these, dare to be enthusiastic. Charge the batteries of those around you, and make dull tasks fun. As you do, many will follow your example, and everything you do will take on its own flavor of success and adventure.

Things to Do Now!

- Smile whenever you're with your friends. Let them know that you're a happy person.

- Speak only positively about your friends, teachers, and leaders. If you have problems with someone, work them out privately.

- Be excited about the work you do! No matter what the task, you're bound to find fun in it somewhere.

- Share your excitement with others! Don't be afraid to show your enthusiasm. By sparking up vigor and energy in your friends you can change a ho-hum group into a dynamic force.

- Find a special battery charger of your own. Make that person's friendship a special one, and draw on his or her zest for life to keep yourself highly charged.

INDEX